The
New Mandarins of
American Power

In Memoriam

Christopher Hill
(1912–2003)

—The—
New Mandarins of
American Power

The Bush Administration's
Plans for the World

— Alex Callinicos —

polity

First published in 2003 by Polity Press in association with Blackwell
Publishing Ltd.

Editorial office:
Polity Press
65 Bridge Street
Cambridge CB2 1UR, UK

Marketing and production:
Blackwell Publishing Ltd
108 Cowley Road
Oxford OX4 1JF, UK

Distributed in the USA by
Blackwell Publishing Inc.
350 Main Street
Malden, MA 02148, USA

A catalogue record for this book is available from the British Library.

Library of Congress Cataloging-in-Publication Data

Callinicos, Alex.
The new mandarins of American power: the Bush administration's plans for
the world / Alex Callinicos.
    p. cm.
Includes bibliographical references and index.
ISBN 0-7456-3274-2 (hb: alk. paper) – ISBN 0-7456-3275-0 (pb: alk. paper)
1. United States—Foreign relations – 2001– 2. United States—Military
policy. 3. Bush, George W. (George Walker), 1946—Political and social
views. 4. Balance of power. 5. War on Terrorism, 2001– 6. Conservatism
—United States. 7. Capitalism—Political aspects. 8. Imperialism. I. Title.
E902.C35 2004
327.73′009′0511 – dc21

                                                                2003013625

Typeset in 11 on 13 pt Sabon
by SNP Best-set Typesetter Ltd., Hong Kong
Printed and bound in Great Britain by MPG Books Ltd, Bodmin, Cornwall

For further information on Polity, visit our website: www.polity.co.uk

Contents

Preface   vii

Acknowledgements   ix

Prologue: At War between the Two Rivers   1

1   The Rhetoric of Conquest   8

Between good and evil   8

Terrorism   11

Rogue states and the axis of evil   14

Weapons of mass destruction   18

Democracy   23

Liberal alibis   34

2   The Cultists of Eternal War   42

The Bush Doctrine   42

Bush II: the Republican right take the helm   44

Chronicle of a war foretold   48

3 The Grand Strategy of the American Empire 54

American strategy after the Cold War 54

Exploiting America's military edge 64

America versus Europe 76

4 The Geopolitics of Oil 80

Remaking the Middle East 80

Blood and oil 93

5 Collision of Empires 99

Imperialism and Empire 99

The peculiarities of American imperialism 106

A return to interimperialist rivalries? 119

Catastrophe immanent 127

Epigraph 131

Notes 132

Index 151

Preface

This book offers a critical analysis of the global strategy pursued by the Bush administration since 11 September 2001. That is a big subject in itself, and so various important and related topics have, of necessity, been largely or wholly ignored. Most notably, the Israeli–Palestinian conflict is dealt with only in passing. A careful and detailed study of the origins, internal dynamics and ideological composition of American neoconservativism would be a most valuable contribution to our understanding of contemporary history: such a task was, however, beyond the remit of this book, not to speak of the limits set by my own capacities. There are also difficult philosophical and political questions about the relationship between cosmopolitanism and sovereignty that I have not addressed. Despite such omissions, I hope that what I have written is of some use.

I owe much to the help of others. An early version of parts of this book first appeared as an article in *International Socialism* in the autumn of 2002. Chris Harman and John Rees provided both advice and sources. I am also very much indebted to Sebastian Budgen, one of whose many roles is as a one-person internet search engine for a small but very lucky network of left-wing intellectuals. In those extraordinary weeks before the outbreak of war on Iraq, I participated in two conferences, one on Retours à Marx at the Collège Internationale de Philosophie in Paris, and the other on Liberalism and Empire at the City University of New York. The discussions there were very helpful in clarifying my thinking on some of the topics covered in this book. Among my interlocutors at these conferences, I am particularly grateful to Daniel Bensaïd, David Harvey and Leo Panitch. I have also benefited from the discussions I have been having with Gilbert Achcar for several years now. Finally, Sam Ashman read this book in draft and subjected it to withering criticism. It is entirely my fault if the book fails to live up to the exacting standards she demanded of it.

At Polity David Held has been a true Mephistopheles, tempting me yet again from the path of virtue. All the same, I am grateful to him for his encouragement, and to everyone else with whom I have dealt at Polity, who have been, as ever, helpful and professional. I would like to thank particularly Ann Bone, Sandra Byatt, Rachel Kerr, Annabelle Mundy and Pam Thomas.

I am dedicating this book to Christopher Hill, the great Marxist historian of seventeenth-century England, who died a few days after the antiwar protests of 15 February 2003. Like many others who passed through Balliol during his mastership in the 1960s and 1970s, I benefited greatly from (though was always rather in awe of) his formidable but benevolent presence, and his writings have been an enormous inspiration. Typically his death was the occasion of a scurrilous Cold War attack in the Murdoch press. But maybe Christopher would have been pleased that the British establishment still regarded him as a foe worth trying to smear. He certainly would have been delighted to know that – as 15 February showed – the Good Old Cause is alive and well.

Acknowledgements

The author and the publishers would like to thank the following for permission to use copyright material:

Financial Times for extracts from D. Gardner, 'Living with the Wolf'; R. Khalaf, 'A Troubled Friendship'; M. Wolf, 'Asia is Footing the Bill for American Guns and Butter' and P. Stephens, 'A Divided Europe will be Easy for America to Rule', from *Financial Times*, 17 Feb. 1998, 22 Aug. 2002, 19 Feb. 2003 and 23 May 2003, © The Financial Times.

Michael Ledeen for an extract from 'The Real Foe is Middle East Tyranny', *Financial Times*, 24 Sept. 2002.

London Review of Books for an extract from A. Lieven, 'The New Cold War', *London Review of Books*, 4 Oct. 2001.

Penguin Books Ltd for extracts from Walter Hamilton's translation of A. Marcellinus, *The Later Roman Empire* (Harmondsworth: Penguin, 1986).

Stratfor for extracts from G. Friedman, 'The Region after Iraq', 6 Feb. 2003, and 'American Isolation and the European Reality', 12 Mar. 2003, www.stratfor.com.

Every effort has been made to trace copyright holders, but if any have been inadvertently overlooked, the publishers will be pleased to make the necessary arrangements at the first opportunity.

Prologue

At War between the Two Rivers

In April AD 363, the Emperor Julian – the last pagan to rule Rome – led an army across the Euphrates, the great river that separated his domain from the rival Persian empire. His target was the Persian capital of Ctesiphon, whose ruins lie about twenty miles south of Baghdad, on the eastern bank of the Tigris.[1] Imperial wars were, of course, even then nothing new in Mesopotamia, the ancient land between the Tigris and the Euphrates where, sometime during the fourth millennium BC, human beings first began to live in cities. Michael Mann calls Sargon of Akkad, who carved out, by conquest, commerce and guile, an extensive empire in Mesopotamia around the turn of the twenty-fourth century BC, 'the first personality in history'.[2] Recorded history began, as it has continued, as the tale of conquerors and rulers.

The best account of Julian's expedition is provided by Ammianus Marcellinus, who served as an officer in the Roman invasion army. He describes the march to Ctesiphon, interspersed with the sieges of cities that fell sometimes by force, sometimes thanks to negotiation. (At one point Julian and his men discovered 'many corpses on gibbets, the family of the man who surrendered the town of Pirisabora'.) At the walls of Ctesiphon itself, Julian found himself confronted with an enemy that refused battle. Deciding that to besiege so large and well fortified a city was not feasible, the emperor led his army further inland, after destroying the fleet that he had used to transport supplies up the Tigris. Ammianus records how

> the enemy set fire to the vegetation and standing crops in order to expose us to the torments of starvation . . . The Persians also began to make game of us from a distance, at one moment spreading themselves out and at the next halting in close order, to give the impression to those watching from afar that the king's forces had arrived, and to make us believe that this accounted for their bold sallies and unusual tactics.[3]

The heavily armoured Roman infantry toiled on in what Ammianus calls 'the almost intolerable heat' of a Middle Eastern summer, struggling with hunger and harassed by Persian cavalry (sometimes supported by elephants). Ammianus comments on these engagements: 'The Persians fell in greater numbers because they often lack spirit in a clash of arms and are at a grave disadvantage in hand-to-hand combat. Their forte is fighting at longer range, and if they see their forces giving ground they deter the enemy from pursuit by discharging a rain of arrows backward as they withdraw.'[4] In one of these skirmishes, Julian was mortally wounded. He died discussing philosophy – as Gibbon suggests, somewhat ostentatiously displaying the pagan virtues he had sought to defend against the rising power of Christianity.[5] Julian's death threatened the Roman army with destruction: his successor Jovian rapidly negotiated a humiliating peace treaty that allowed the Romans to retreat back across the Euphrates in exchange for the surrender of five provinces and a key border city.

In March 2003 two of the Western states that trace their origins back to the civilization of classical antiquity so long ruled by Rome launched another military expedition in

Mesopotamia – or, as it has been known since the partition of the Ottoman Empire after the First World War, the modern Arab state of Iraq. The war waged by the United States and Britain against Iraq had echoes of that invasion mounted by Julian 1,640 years earlier, as heavily armed Anglo-American troops struggled with an inhospitable terrain, fighting an enemy that was most effective when it refused open battle and used unconventional tactics instead. There were, however, important differences.

First and most obvious: where Julian had failed, George W. Bush and Tony Blair succeeded. Unlike its ancient neighbour Ctesiphon, modern Baghdad fell to the invaders. The widespread looting that followed while the occupying forces looked on would have been familiar to those involved in older wars. Indeed, the theft and destruction of antiquities in the Iraq Museum in Baghdad – a cultural catastrophe of world-historic proportions – recalled an earlier disaster, when the city was sacked by the Mongols in 1258. Commenting on the looting in the House of Commons, Geoff Hoon, the British Defence Secretary, said: 'I regard such behaviour as good practice perhaps.'[6] But the victorious political and military chiefs conducted themselves very differently from Julian, whose death was a direct consequence of a style of leadership plainly modelled on the heroic generalship of Alexander the Great: as Ammianus admiringly puts it, 'he would give his men confidence by fighting in the front rank.'[7] Conforming to what John Keegan calls the modern norm of 'post-heroic leadership', the American and British commanders directed the battle far from the front, carefully insulated from danger in heavily fortified and guarded situation rooms that were developed in the nuclear era to foil an enemy 'strategy of decapitation'.[8] The Commander in Chief himself took this style to extremes: after telling the camera crews filming his announcement of the outbreak of hostilities on 20 March 2003: 'I feel good,' George W. Bush took off for a long weekend at Camp David. The enemy leader was afforded no such security: indeed, the

Anglo-American attack began with a flurry of cruise missiles avowedly planned as a 'decapitation strike' against the Iraqi Ba'athist regime intended to kill Saddam Hussein and his sons.

And here, in the nature of the belligerent regimes, lies, apparently, the greatest difference. Julian's invasion of Persia in 363 was an incident in the long struggle between the two rival empires, a contest that lasted four centuries, until the Bedouin armies of Islam took advantage of a moment when both sides were exhausted from a particularly savage bout of warfare to sweep away the Persian monarchy and conquer most of the Roman Empire's possessions in the Near East. The Iraq War of 2003, by contrast, pitted two liberal democracies against an authoritarian pan-Arabist regime with a particularly savage history of repression that left it with few defenders. Theirs was a war of liberation, the American president and the British prime minister constantly insisted.

More than that, it was a war for democracy – not simply to remedy injustice but to institute a just social and political order. A few weeks before hostilities began, President Bush compared his administration's plans for Iraq and indeed for the Middle East as a whole with the establishment of liberal democracies in Japan and West Germany under American occupation after the Second World War:

> The current Iraqi regime has shown the power of tyranny to spread discord and violence in the Middle East. A liberated Iraq can show the power of freedom to transform that vital region, by bringing hope and progress into the lives of millions . . . There was a time when many said that the cultures of Japan and Germany were incapable of sustaining democratic values. Well, they were wrong. Some say the same of Iraq today. They are mistaken. (Applause.) The nation of Iraq – with its proud heritage, abundant resources and skilled and educated people – is fully capable of moving toward democracy and living in freedom. (Applause.)[9]

On 3 April 2003, as American forces penetrated Baghdad, James Woolsey, former Director of Central Intelligence and one of the strongest advocates of war on Iraq, addressed a teach-in at UCLA organized by 'Americans for Victory over Terrorism'. Woolsey announced that the United States was engaged in World War IV. (The Cold War, apparently, had been the Third World War.) He said: 'This fourth world war, I think, will last considerably longer than either World Wars I or II did for us. Hopefully not the full four-plus decades of the Cold War.' The Bush administration wasn't just fighting terrorism, Woolsey explained; it was engaged in a struggle to create 'a new Middle East', spreading democracy to prevent hostile Muslim and Arab forces from destroying liberal civilization. He warned the Saudi royal family and President Hosni Mubarak of Egypt: 'We want you to realize now, for the fourth time in a hundred years, this country and its allies are on the march and that we are on the side of those whom you . . . most fear: We're on the side of your own people.'[10] Karl Rove, Bush's main political strategist, took the same line: 'It's the battle of Iraq, not the war . . . This is part of the war on terrorism.'[11] Two of the neo-conservatives whose views seem increasingly dominant in Washington wrote before Iraq's conquest: 'The mission begins in Baghdad, but it does not end there . . . Duly armed, the United States can act to secure its safety and to advance the cause of liberty – in Baghdad and beyond.'[12] Such remarks are symptomatic of the millenarian outlook of key figures in and around the Bush administration. The 'war on terrorism' began as a response to the attacks on New York and Washington on 11 September 2001. Whatever one thinks about the form taken by this response, it was an intelligible reaction to a specific and demonstrable threat. Now it has become a global and permanent state of war that will last longer than the two most terrible military conflicts in the history of humankind and whose rationale is a project of sociopolitical transformation – the use of the military power of the United States to impose 'democratic values' on parts of the world that are identified as threats to 'liberal civilization'. As the philosopher Giorgio Agamben put it, 'the White House is trying to impose on its country and on the planet as a whole a permanent state of emergency [*un état d'exception permanent*], which is presented to us as a response to a kind of global civil war between the state and terrorism.'[13]

This is hardly a hidden agenda. On the contrary, it is proclaimed publicly, not merely by neoconservative ideologues, but in what amounts to the Bush administration's war manifesto, *The National Security Strategy of the United States of America*, published in September 2002. As for the aim, it is well expressed in the name of a key neoconservative pressure group: The Project for the New American Century. The definite article is significant – *the* New American Century. This is about shaping the world for the next hundred years according to the interests and values of American free-market capitalism. It would seem an important, indeed an urgent task to understand the nature of this project, its ideological justifications, inner coherence, and motivating forces.

Such is the aim of this short book. Its structure reflects these objectives. In chapter 1, I critically consider the ideological discourse used to justify the war on terrorism. Chapter 2 links together the operative conclusion of this discourse – the Bush Doctrine of preventive war – with the political team of neoconservatives who are its authors. I analyse the broader geostrategy that the Bush administration is pursuing in chapter 3 and its specific objectives in the Middle East in chapter 4 before, in the final chapter, situating this project in the larger history of imperialism.

This book uses the methods of scholarship, but it is not a detached inquiry. It is written more in fulfilment of the duties of citizenship, as the terrifying military apparatus deployed on the banks of the Tigris commands the world to accept a permanent state of emergency till the programme devised by its political masters has been fulfilled.

The book's title echoes that of Noam Chomsky's classic *American Power and the New Mandarins* (1969) – partly in tribute to the stance of unflinching opposition to American imperialism that Chomsky has maintained for more than a generation without surrendering the highest of intellectual standards. His kind of rigorous critique is required now more than ever.

Though fear is a natural emotion to feel at present, it is not the only, or even the main one motivating this book. The prospect and the actuality of war on Iraq provoked the explosion of what is without doubt the greatest international protest movement in world history. In particular the global day of action on the eve of war, on 15 February 2003, is simply without any precedent. Within the space of eighteen months – from the first demonstrations against the war on Afghanistan in the autumn of 2001 to the torrent of protest in the spring of 2003 – a worldwide antiwar movement far greater than that against the Vietnam War sprang into existence. The protests of 15 February registered even on the radar of the deeply conservative and cautious *New York Times*, which commented: 'The fracturing of the Western alliance over Iraq and the huge anti-war demonstrations around the world this weekend are reminders that there may still be two superpowers on the planet: the United States and world public opinion.'[14]

So I write in the hope evoked by the rise of this second superpower. If the 'war on terrorism' really is the global, decade-long struggle that its architects proclaim it to be, then the movement against it will have to be a long-term campaign as well. To be effective, resistance will have to be informed by an understanding of the strange and frightening world in which we find ourselves living. This book is a small contribution to that understanding.

– 1 –

The Rhetoric of Conquest

Between good and evil

The Bush administration made two critical ideological moves in the days following the terrorist atrocities of 11 September 2001. First, it proclaimed itself to be at war. Despite endless chatter about the novelty and asymmetric character of this war, the effect was to make a reasonable end – ensuring that nothing like the 9/11 outrages happened again – dependent on the exercise of military power. Proclaiming a state of war (though without engaging in the quaint constitutional and diplomatic niceties of formally declaring war on any other states) also had the beneficial side-effect of justifying emergency measures limiting or even denying altogether the exercise of civil liberties: the most extreme case of these measures to date is the confinement of prisoners from the Afghan War as 'unlawful combatants' outside the range of the US courts in Guantanamo Bay.

Secondly, the administration defined this war in Manichean terms: 'This will be a monumental struggle between good and evil,' said George W. Bush on 12 September 2001. 'But good will prevail.'[1] If Osama bin

Laden represented absolute evil, then by implication the American way of life embodied its opposite. Constructing the crisis as a clash of moral absolutes then made it easy to demand that everyone choose sides, as Bush famously did in his speech to Congress a few days later: 'Every nation, in every region, now has a decision to make. Either you are with us, or you are with the terrorists.'[2] A primarily moral interpretation of the conflict not only justified this intimidating language, it also closed off any attempt to analyse its causes. Perhaps the most powerful effort to provide a historical perspective on terrorist attacks against the United States actually appeared before 9/11. In *Blowback*, the highly regarded (and hitherto very mainstream) American scholar Chalmers Johnson argued that policies designed to maintain 'a global military-economic dominion' by the United States were producing more and more cases of blowback – a term introduced by the Central Intelligence Agency to refer to 'the unintended consequences of policies that were kept secret from the American people':

Terrorism by definition strikes at the innocent in order to draw attention to the sins of the invulnerable. The innocent of the twenty-first century are going to harvest unexpected blowback disasters from the imperialist escapades of recent decades. Although most Americans may be largely ignorant of what was, and still is, being done in their name, all are likely to pay a steep price – individually and collectively – for their nation's continued efforts to dominate the global scene.[3]

An insight into the political morality responsible for blowback is provided by a remarkable interview that Zbigniew Brzezinski, National Security Advisor to President Jimmy Carter (1977–81), gave in 1998. Here he proudly revealed that Carter had instructed the CIA on 3 July 1979 to give secret aid to the mujahedin, the Islamist guerrillas fighting the Soviet-backed regime in

Afghanistan. Brzezinski recalled that he had told Carter that same day that 'in my opinion this aid was going to induce a Soviet military intervention' – a prediction that was fulfilled in December 1979. It was, of course, out of the subsequent ten-year war that there emerged the radical Islamist networks that Osama bin Laden forged into al-Qaeda and that, in the shape of the Taliban, seized power in Afghanistan in the mid-1990s. Invited to express regret about the consequences of this policy, Brzezinski responded indignantly:

> Regret what? The secret operation was an excellent idea. It had the effect of drawing the Russians into the Afghan trap and you want me to regret it? The day that the Soviets officially crossed the border I wrote to President Carter: we now have the opportunity of giving the USSR its own Vietnam War . . . What is more important to the history of the world? The Taliban or the collapse of the Soviet empire? A few crazed Muslims or the liberation of Central Europe and the end of the Cold War?[4]

World history will surely deliver different answers to Brzezinski's questions from those that he obviously expected. But if 11 September ushered in a struggle between absolute good and evil, then any enquiry into its actual causes was not simply beside the point, but was a typically liberal effort to relativize the values at stake out of existence. 'Moral equivalence' – the accusation that any effort to understand the context of the wars in Palestine, Afghanistan or Iraq amounted to the attempt to equate what are in fact moral opposites – this was the idiot phrase used again and again by the American right to shout down critics after the destruction of the Twin Towers. As if historical and political analysis cannot combine a careful exploration of the causes of great and terrible events with discriminating moral judgement that seeks to distribute responsibility among all the actors implicated in producing them.[5] But then care and discrimination were precisely what the apostles of the 'war on terrorism' were trying to eliminate from public debate. The damaging effect on the quality of political understanding can be seen in the fact, regularly reported in opinion surveys, that a majority of the American public believed at the time of the Iraq War that Saddam Hussein was implicated in the 9/11 attacks, despite the complete absence of any serious evidence linking him to al-Qaeda. The struggle to counter these efforts to pollute serious debate may be helped if – as a preliminary to a close analysis of the Bush administration's strategy – we take a brief critical look at some of the key ideological terms that they have used to justify the 'lengthy campaign' that the President promised Congress after 9/11.

Terrorism

'Terrorism' is, of course, a notoriously slippery term. This is not because, as is sometimes claimed, it is impossible to arrive at an agreed definition. Noam Chomsky, the greatest contemporary critic of American foreign policy, cheerfully adopts the US Army's definition of terrorism as 'the calculated use of violence to attain goals that are political, religious, or ideological in nature . . . through intimidation, coercion, or instilling fear'.[6] The problem with the official discourse of terrorism is not this kind of definition, but partly, as Chomsky has relentlessly pointed out, the selectivity with which it is applied. To take one example that has particular resonance in the Arab world: in the summer of 1982 the Israel Defence Force besieged Beirut. In the course of two and a half months, the IDF indiscriminately rained various kinds of weapons, including phosphorus shells and cluster bombs, on the city. Over 4,000 people were killed in Beirut alone, many of them non-combatants. In September, after the siege had been raised, Christian fascist militiamen massacred at least 700 Palestinian civilians at the Sabra and Chatila refugee camps while their allies in the

IDF looked on. It is hard to think of a more clear-cut case of terrorism as defined by the US Army: the siege was partly intended to force the Arab governments to consent to the expulsion of the Palestine Liberation Organization from Lebanon. Yet Ariel Sharon, as Israeli Minister of Defence the architect of the invasion of Lebanon and condemned by an official commission for allowing the Sabra and Chatila massacres to take place, has been Prime Minister of Israel since 2001 and a key ally of the United States in the 'war on terrorism'.[7]

Such inconsistency in applying the term 'terrorism' is one of the main reasons why so many people around the world – the majority of them neither Arabs nor Muslims – have opposed the 'war on terrorism'. But the problem is not simply that the concept is selectively invoked but that it is promiscuously extended. Two examples may serve to illustrate the point. Take first the Terrorism Act 2000, passed by the British Parliament before 9/11 but one of the inspirations of the absurdly named USA Patriot Act rushed through Congress after the attacks on New York and Washington. This piece of legislation, which greatly extends police powers – for example, allowing detention of suspects without trial for up to seven days – defines terrorism, in the words of the civil rights organization Liberty, as

> any act or threat of action which involves serious violence against a person or serious damage to property, endangers a person's life (but not just the life of the person committing the act), creates a serious risk to the health or safety of the public or, finally, is designed to seriously interfere with or disrupt an electronic system. Any such act must furthermore be 'designed to influence or to intimidate the public or a section of the public', and to further the advancement of a 'political, religious, or ideological cause'.[8]

As Liberty points out, this is an 'extremely vague' definition, particularly in that it extends terrorism to include actions that threaten property. Consequently, 'it is capable of encompassing activities which whilst unlawful cannot properly be regarded as terrorism e.g. animal rights activism or even in certain circumstances civil disobedience e.g. tree protestors, or even some forms of industrial action.'[9] The Act also creates a new crime of inciting terrorism overseas that, if in force before 1990, could have made anyone who spoke in solidarity with Nelson Mandela and others involved in the African National Congress's campaign of armed struggle against apartheid liable to life imprisonment.[10] The discourse of counterterrorism may also affect the conduct of war itself. It was noticeable during the invasion of Iraq that American and British military spokespeople – and, even worse, supposedly 'objective' media organizations such as the BBC – would describe actions by Iraqi irregulars as 'acts of terrorism' and the units involved as 'death squads'. Yet these were armed attacks on US and British military personnel who had invaded Iraq. If these were terrorist acts then it appears that the mere act of resisting the forces of good in the 'war on terrorism' itself counts as terrorism.

One might respond to such criticisms by agreeing that the term 'terrorism' is frequently misused, but insisting nonetheless that 9/11 was undoubtedly an example of the phenomenon in question and one that required a military response to prevent anything like it happening again. This reply might seem, on the face of it, perfectly reasonable, but it begs two questions. First, is it really the case that the strategy pursued by the Bush administration will make further terrorist attacks on the United States and its allies less likely? This is, of course, something strongly contested, for example, by critics of the war on Iraq. Even as loyal a client of Washington as the Egyptian President Hosni Mubarak warned that, as a result of the war, 'we will have a hundred bin Ladens.'[11] The suicide bombings mounted by al-Qaeda and its allies in Saudi Arabia and Morocco in May 2003, shortly after the conquest of Iraq, would seem to corroborate this prediction. But, secondly and more radically, is the primary concern behind the Bush strategy that of eradicating terrorism? The rest of this book will seek to show that this question should be answered in the negative. While the Bush administration undoubtedly does want to destroy al-Qaeda and its like, it is pursuing a much larger geopolitical agenda. This is one reason why the discourse of terrorism should be approached with such suspicion.

Rogue states and the axis of evil

Critical in widening the focus of the 'war on terrorism' has, of course, been the policy of associating terrorism with states that are then presented as legitimate targets of military action. The key step here came with the substantial extension of war aims announced by Bush in his State of the Union address on 29 January 2002. Reaffirming that 'our war on terror is just beginning', he announced that, in addition to directly attacking terrorist networks, 'our second goal is to prevent regimes that sponsor terror from threatening America or our friends and allies with weapons of mass destruction', and named Iran, Iraq and North Korea as 'an axis of evil'.[12] Under Secretary of State John Bolton subsequently extended the net, identifying Libya, Syria and Cuba as 'state sponsors of terrorism that are pursuing or who have the potential to pursue weapons of mass destruction'.[13]

The idea of an *axis* of evil doesn't stand up to a moment's examination. It refers implicitly to the Axis that bound together Germany, Japan and Italy during the Second World War. But this was a formal military alliance that sought legitimacy in the ideology of the interwar extreme right (it originated in the Anti-Comintern Pact of November 1936). But no alliance bound together Iran, Iraq and North Korea. Iran and Iraq fought one of the bloodiest wars of the late twentieth century between 1980 and 1988; the Islamic Republican regime in Tehran took an equivocal attitude towards the destruction of its Ba'athist rival. North Korea occupies a completely different geographical region and is ruled by a Stalinist autocracy notorious for its suspicion of outside contact. There is, moreover, little ideologically in common between Shi'ite radical Islamism, secular pan-Arab nationalism, and jucheism, the North Korean variant of Marxism–Leninism centred on the idea of self-reliance (*chuch'e*).

The usable kernel of the idea of the axis of evil is that staple of official US discourse, the concept of rogue states. This rests on a kind of sociopolitical pathology – that of 'failed' states that are unable to provide their own subjects with minimum standards of 'good governance' and that therefore constitute a threat to their neighbours and to the 'international community' at large (I apologize for the numerous quotation marks: they are a sign that we are dealing with a discourse many of whose terms cry out for deconstruction). This pathology is, as one would expect, parasitic on a conception of normality one key element of which is the idea of the 'democratic peace' – in other words, the theory (hotly contested among international relations specialists) that liberal democracies do not go to war with one another.[14] The connection between a defective internal regime and dangerous external behaviour has three critical functions. First and most obviously, it offers an explanation for the faults of the state in question that does not implicate outside forces. Secondly, it justifies external intervention to overturn authoritarian regimes, since the denial of democracy does not merely injure their own citizens but is a source of danger to outsiders. Finally, the explanation implies that intervention can only reliably remove this threat if it produces a project of political transformation that roots democracy in the failed society.

I return to the idea of externally imposed democratic revolution below. For the time being I want to look more closely at the external manifestations through which a rogue state makes itself known. In a fascinating discussion of the etymology of the word '*voyou*', used in France to translate 'rogue', Jacques Derrida has shown how *'voyou'* has resonances of the werewolf and the outlaw and also of plebeian banditry that threatens public and moral order. He suggests: 'We discover a homologous structure when we speak of these states that are called rogue, denounced, fought, and repressed by the policing of the states that proclaim themselves legitimate and respectful of an international law they have the power to control.'[15]

As this analysis suggests, central to the concept of rogue states is the notion of outlawry. The rogue state places itself outside the international community by the contempt it shows for international law. After their failure in February–March 2003 to win a resolution by the United Nations Security Council authorizing an attack on Iraq, the US and British governments fell back in justification of their unilateral action on Saddam Hussein's alleged violation of eighteen other Security Council resolutions. Despite *their* flouting of the UN, Washington and London insisted, *he* was the outlaw. But this argument invited the *tu quoque* response given by Derrida before the fact that 'the most *rogue* of *rogue states* are those that put in circulation and to work a concept like that of *rogue state*, with the language, the rhetoric, the juridical discourse and the strategico-military consequences that we know.'[16]

Derrida draws here on the more detailed argument of Noam Chomsky. But a very similar case has been made by Samuel Huntington, one of the pillars of the US national security establishment. During the second Clinton administration Huntington described America's increasing international isolation:

On issue after issue, the United States has found itself increasingly alone, with one or fewer partners, opposing most of the rest of the world's states and peoples. These issues include UN dues; sanctions against Cuba, Iran, Iraq, and Libya; the land mines treaty; global warming; an international war crimes tribunal; the Middle East; the use of force against Iraq and Yugoslavia; and the targeting of 35 countries with new economic sanctions between 1993 and 1996. On these and other issues, much of the international community is on one side and the United States is on the other. The circle of governments who see their interests coinciding with American interests is shrinking. This is manifest, among other ways, in the central line-up among the permanent members of the UN Security Council. During the first decades of the Cold War, it was 4:1 – the United States, the United Kingdom, France, and China against the Soviet Union. After Mao's communist government took China's seat, the line-up became 3:1:1, with China in a shifting middle position. Now it is 2:1:2, with the United States and the United Kingdom opposing China and Russia, and France in the middle spot.

While the United States regularly denounces various countries as 'rogue states', in the eyes of many countries it is becoming the rogue superpower.[17]

Huntington's diagnosis is all the more remarkable because it was written under the Clinton administration – now regarded by many with nostalgia as a beacon of multilateralism, and by its neoconservative critics as the epitome of 'wishful liberalism'.[18] Huntington's article appeared in March 1999, when its analysis was confirmed by the US decision to lead a Nato attack on Serbia without the authority of the Security Council. Under George W. Bush, the American shift towards unilateralism has been radicalized with the administration's denunciation of the Kyoto protocol on global warming, the treaty establishing an International Criminal Court, and the Anti-Ballistic Missile Treaty, and its prosecution of the 'war on terrorism' through 'coalitions of the willing' rather than within the framework of Nato, let alone the UN. The international debate on war with Iraq represented a further step in the pattern of isolation described by Huntington. On the one hand, the efforts of the Bush administration to win a resolution authorizing military action, loyally if ineptly seconded by the government of Tony Blair in Britain, provoked the formation of a powerful antiwar bloc on the Security Council comprising two permanent members, France and Russia, and the most important European state, Germany; on the other hand, the US could not even win the support of its two partners in the North American Free Trade Agreement, Canada and Mexico, or of Turkey, a key Near Eastern ally whose refusal to allow its territory to be used for attacking Iraq greatly complicated Anglo-American military operations. The net effect was fundamentally to compromise the attempts of the US – and perhaps even more stridently Britain – to present themselves as exemplars of democratic normality and the agents of the international community in bringing outlaws to justice. In the eyes of many international jurists it was they who had placed themselves outside that community by waging an illegal war.[19]

Weapons of mass destruction

The fall-back position justifying the prosecution of war without UN authority by the US was the threat represented by the states it attacked. Article 51 of the Charter of the United Nations affirms 'the inherent right of individual or collective self-defence if an armed attack occurs against a member of the United Nations'. Some commentators have long pointed out that this clause, in combination with the permanent members' right of veto over Security Council resolutions, fatally compromises the Charter's promise of collective security by leaving questions of war and peace to what Hans Morgenthau called 'the decentralization of law enforcement' – in other words the initiative of individual states in an anarchic international system.[20] During the invasion of Iraq 'the inherent right of self-defence' was even invoked by US military spokesmen to justify American soldiers shooting civilians whom they mistakenly believed to be a threat to them.

But the serious form taken by the threat that was held to justify unilateral action was the alleged possession by targeted states of weapons of mass destruction (WMD) – in other words, nuclear, chemical and biological weapons. Bush's 'axis of evil' speech made the link explicitly. A key element in the Anglo-American case for war in Iraq was Saddam's alleged failure to rid himself of WMD as required by Security Council resolutions passed during the 1991 Gulf War. This was part of a larger attempt to portray the Iraqi regime as a uniquely expansionist state that was a serious threat to both regional and global peace. The Ba'athist regime's gassing of thousands of Kurds at Halabja in northern Iraq in March 1988, during the first Gulf War, between Iran and Iraq, was frequently cited as evidence of Saddam's wickedness and also to show, as John Mearsheimer and Stephen Walt put it, that 'Saddam is a warped human being who might use WMD without regard for the consequences'. Mearsheimer and Walt, like Huntington leading American policy intellectuals, continue:

> Unfortunately for those who now favour war, this argument is difficult to reconcile with the United States's past support for Iraq, support that coincided with some of the behaviour now being invoked to portray him as an irrational madman. The United States backed Iraq during the 1980s – when Saddam was gassing Kurds and Iranians – and helped Iraq use chemical weapons by providing it with satellite imagery of Iranian troop positions. The Reagan administration also facilitated Iraq's efforts to develop biological weapons by allowing Baghdad to import disease-producing biological materials such as anthrax, West Nile virus, and botulinal toxin. A central figure in the effort to court Iraq was none other than current Defense Secretary Donald Rumsfeld, who was then President Ronald Reagan's special envoy to the Middle East. He visited Baghdad and met with Saddam in 1983, with the explicit aim of fostering better relations between the United States and Iraq. In October 1989, about a year after Saddam gassed the Kurds, President George H. W. Bush signed a formal national security directive declaring, 'Normal relations between the United States and Iraq

would promote our longer-term interests and promote stability in both the Gulf and the Middle East.'[21]

Rumsfeld in fact met Saddam twice in 1983–4. At their first meeting, on 21 December 1983, the two men agreed that the US and Iraq had a common interest in preventing an outcome to the Iran–Iraq War that 'weakened Iraq's role or enhanced interests or ambitions of Iran'. The US and Iraq resumed diplomatic relations (which Baghdad had broken off during the 1967 Arab–Israeli War) in November 1984 despite the fact that Washington was well aware that Iraq was developing and using chemical weapons against Iran.[22] The British government displayed even greater indifference to Saddam's methods, doubling its export credits to Iraq from £175 million in 1987 to £340 million in 1988. A secret Ministry of Defence report declared in June 1988, three months after Halabja: 'UK Ltd is helping Iraq, often unwillingly, but sometimes not, to set up a major indigenous arms industry.'[23]

Granted that Saddam was a monster, he had been, during the 1980s, when Western policy in the Middle East was dominated by the imperative of isolating and weakening the Iranian Revolution, 'our' monster. Had he used WMD against the US and its allies in either the 1991 or the 2003 wars, it would then have been a spectacular case of blowback. In the event, he did not – despite Tony Blair's claim in September 2002 that he had 'existing and active military plans for the use of chemical and biological weapons, which could be activated within 45 minutes'.[24] The dossiers constructed by the British government and used by the US State Department to justify the Iraq War proved under examination to rest on extremely dodgy evidence. The second dossier, produced in February 2003, became the subject of widespread derision when it was revealed that it included plagiarized (and distorted) excerpts from an article based on a Ph.D. thesis. The first, which appeared in September 2002, contained the serious, and widely repeated allegation that Iraq had sought in

1999–2001 to import from Niger 500 tones of uranium oxide, which could have been processed to provide weapons-grade uranium for dozens of nuclear bombs. In March 2003 the UN International Atomic Energy Agency dismissed the documents substantiating this claim as a palpable forgery. The inaccuracies were so obvious, according to one official, that 'they could be spotted by someone using Google on the Internet'. Past and present US and UN officials suggested to the investigative journalist Seymour Hersh that the documents might have been produced as part of a black propaganda operation mounted against Iraq in the late 1990s by the British Secret Intelligence Service, MI6.[25] More startlingly, in May 2003 the BBC quoted a senior intelligence official who said that the dossier had been 'transformed' on the orders of Blair's office to make it 'sexier'. The claim for example that Iraqi WMD were ready for use within forty-five minutes 'was not in the original draft. It was included in the dossier against our wishes because it wasn't reliable.'[26] The source for this report proved to be Dr David Kelly, a senior Ministry of Defence expert on chemical and biological warfare. His apparent suicide in July 2003 threw the Blair government into its most serious crisis to date. From such dubious evidence came the arguments to justify plunging the Middle East into war.

The issue of weapons of mass destruction raises much larger questions about the nature of the international system. The proliferation of WMD is undeniably a major threat to the future of humankind. But neither Washington's definition of the problem nor its solution are of any help in addressing the threat. For one thing equating WMD with nuclear, chemical and biological weapons tacitly legitimizes the highly destructive 'conventional' weapons increasingly monopolized by the Pentagon. For another, the nuclear status quo is treated as the norm from which deviations are to be suppressed. This status quo has two features. First, the open, acknowledged possession of nuclear weapons by the five permanent Security Council members, with the US (12,070 nuclear warheads) and Russia (22,500 nuclear warheads) overwhelmingly in the lead.[27] Second, the development of nuclear weapons by more minor powers – notably Israel, whose capability to deliver several hundred nuclear warheads is one of the worst kept secrets of international politics, but is held not to be a breach of normality requiring intervention because of Israel's close alliance with the US; and India and Pakistan, whose nuclear tests in 1998 evoked sanctions from the US that were abandoned after 9/11 because of the significance of those countries as allies in the 'war on terrorism' in Afghanistan.

A key objective in this war is to prevent the further spread of WMD, especially by 'rogue states'. The most immediate case in question is that of North Korea, whose rulers provoked an international crisis in the winter of 2002–3 by resuming their nuclear programme and withdrawing from the Nuclear Non-Proliferation Treaty. The moral position of the US on this question is weak given that it introduced nuclear weapons into South Korea in the late 1950s in violation of the armistice agreement that ended the 1950–3 war. Nevertheless in 1993–4 the Clinton administration seriously contemplated a pre-emptive strike against North Korea because of fears that P'yŏngyang had started a weapons programme at its Yŏngbyŏn nuclear facility. In the event the crisis was ended by the so-called Agreed Framework settled in October 1994, under which the North Korean regime agreed to suspend operations at Yŏngbyŏn in exchange for economic assistance by a consortium including the US, Japan and South Korea, in particular to develop a non-military nuclear programme of light-water reactors.[28] The implementation of this alternative programme was, however, much delayed. The Bush administration made its distaste for the Agreed Framework plain from the start, and, of course, included North Korea in the axis of evil – a move that infuriated China, Japan and South Korea since it threatened further to destabilize an already tense region. One does not have to have any time for the North Korean regime and its leader Kim Jong-Il to recognize a certain instrumental rationality in their decision to reactivate their own nuclear programme in order to extract economic and security concessions from a Washington preoccupied with Iraq.[29]

Even a decision to develop nuclear weapons (it is possible that North Korea already has a couple) can't be dismissed as simply irrational. The comparison between Kim Jong-Il's survival and Saddam's destruction may encourage other states to draw the conclusion that, as Lawrence Freedman put it, 'the only apparently credible way to deter the armed force of the US is to own your own nuclear arsenal.'[30] Of course, any attempt to mount a nuclear attack on the US itself would provoke a devastating response, but the capability to threaten neighbouring states (even with conventional weapons North Korea has the capacity to inflict carnage in the city of Seoul) is undoubtedly a significant bargaining chip. Were North Korean possession of a nuclear capability to be confirmed one highly probable consequence would be decisions by Japan and South Korea themselves to develop nuclear weapons – a response that has already been advocated by some American conservatives.[31] US failure to implement the Agreed Framework and the reckless inclusion of North Korea in the axis of evil would then have added a nuclear dimension to the arms race that has developed in North East Asia over the past decade or so. In other words, Washington's policies are calculated to encourage the further proliferation of weapons of mass destruction.

Democracy

The ideology of the 'war on terrorism' is not, however, defined simply by the threats to which it supposedly seeks to respond. As we have already seen, increasingly it has been presented as embracing a positive objective, namely the extension of democracy. Regime change in Iraq was justified not simply by the removal of a rogue state but by the establishment of a democratic polity in its place. For the authors of this ideology, the adoption of this objective is intelligible only against the background of the spread of liberal democracies over the past three decades – to Southern Europe in the 1970s, Latin America in the 1980s, Eastern and Central Europe and South Africa in the 1990s. As the Stalinist regimes started to collapse, Francis Fukuyama proclaimed the End of History in the triumph of liberal capitalism. For the ideologues of the Republican right, liberal democracy – undergirded, as we shall see, by free-market capitalism – is undeniably the end of history in the sense of the goal towards which it is moving.

Democratization does not, however, seem to be a universal objective of the Bush administration. Thus in Central Asia it has closely allied itself to the regime of Islam Karimov in Uzbekistan, despite the numerous violations of human rights for which the latter is responsible. For example, Amnesty International reported in October 2001 'a worrying rise in the number of reports of arbitrary detentions, ill-treatment and torture, in particular of individuals suspected by the Uzbek authorities to be supporters of or sympathizers with Islamic opposition parties', the creation of 'strict regime prison camps' for political offenders, and the forced resettlement of thousands of ethnic Tajiks.[32] After 9/11, writes Dana Priest, Uzbekistan nevertheless 'became the regional hub for a new network of US bases in Central Asia'.[33] According to Human Rights Watch, the Karimov regime – the recipient of $189 million in US aid in 2002 – continues to intern between 6,500 and 7,000 political prisoners, to torture, and to rig trials.[34] Similarly, to persuade Pakistan to come on side against what had previously been its clients in the Taliban, Washington poured money into the bankrupt military dictatorship of Pervez Musharraf, and cast a blind eye at the rigged plebiscite that turned him into an 'elected' president in April 2002.[35] The long-standing pattern in which America's imperial democracy sustains compliant Third World dictatorships turns out not to have been merely a feature of the Cold War that can now be discarded.

Let us, however, set such inconsistencies aside for the moment, and take the Bush administration's democratic professions at face value. The critical example that it invokes when seeking to find a model for its programme of 'democratic revolution' – not just in Iraq, but more widely in the Middle East – is provided by the transformation after the Second World War of the defeated Axis powers into liberal democracies firmly integrated into the US-led Western bloc. The attraction of these examples to the architects of the war on Iraq is obvious: the transformation was undertaken against the background of American (and in the German case, British and French) military occupation. 'After defeating enemies, we did not leave behind occupying armies, we left constitutions and parliaments . . .' Bush boasted. 'In societies that once bred fascism and militarism, liberty found a permanent home.'[36] The President got his facts a little wrong here: nearly sixty years after the end of the Second World War, there is still a significant US military presence in both Japan and Germany, which is a matter of great controversy, particularly on the island of Okinawa. All the same, one gets the point: both countries seem to be cases where military occupation had beneficent consequences. Two leading neoconservative intellectuals, Lawrence Kaplan and William Kristol, put the argument in a general form:

> democracy is a political choice, an act of will. Someone, not something, must create it. Often that someone is a single leader – a Lech Walensa, a King Juan Carlos, a Vaclav Havel. Other times, the pressure for democracy comes from a political opposition movement – the African National Congress in South Africa, Solidarity in Poland, or the marchers in Tiananmen Square. But history suggests it comes most effectively from the United States.[37]

This is more than a Great Man, it's a Great Country view of history in which the great mass movements for democratic rights that were such a striking feature of the last decades of the twentieth century are reduced to a walk-on role, with the benign intervention of Washington occupying centre-stage. But is democracy something that can be imposed by force even by the most powerful of states – can it come through the gun-barrel of an Abrams tank? The German and Japanese cases might suggest that it can: an occupying army can provide the coercive power to root out the authoritarian institutions responsible for 'fascism and militarism' and promote a democratic political culture. This seems, however, an enormous oversimplification. Let us note first the geopolitical context of the liberal-democratic reconstruction of Japan and West Germany – a developing Cold War that gave the US a strong incentive to create counterweights to the USSR in what had been the most powerful military and industrial centres in East Asia and continental Europe before their defeat in 1945.

John Dower in his outstanding history of Japan under the US occupation (1945–52) writes: 'Post-war Japan was a vastly freer and more egalitarian nation than imperial Japan was.' Nevertheless, he stresses that 'the victors also were responsible for strengthening the already powerful bureaucratic authoritarianism they encountered.' Thus 'the "reverse course"' – the shift in American policy towards Japan prompted by the developing confrontation with the USSR – 'helped to establish a domestic hegemony of politicians, bureaucrats and businessmen that remained dominant to the end of the century'.[38] Japan today is governed by what amounts to a one-party regime – not in the sense that other parties are repressed, but that only one party governs. The Liberal Democratic Party has held office almost continuously since 1955 as the apex of a political system that binds together the state bureaucracy, the great *keiretsu* business empires linking banks and industrial corporations, and local oligarchies in a cluster of alliances that is regulated by arcane inner-party factional manoeuvres but that has proved almost impervious to external pressure, as is indicated by the catastrophic paralysis of economic policy in the face of the deflationary slump that has held Japan in its grip since the early 1990s. The Federal Republic of Germany, by contrast, has enjoyed genuine and lively political competition since its establishment in 1949. This reflects the fact that the Western occupying powers found important local partners in the shape of two of the three main sociopolitical forces that proved most resistant to the National Socialist regime – the predominantly Social-Democratic labour movement and the Catholic *Zentrum*. (The third, the Communist Party, provided the East German state with its political base and continues to exert an influence in reunified Germany through its ultimate heir, the Party of Democratic Socialism.)

These historical examples support the truism that any attempt to graft new political forms onto a society from the outside will fail unless it can find suitable domestic allies. Whether they exist in Iraq, for example, in a form acceptable to the Bush administration, is extremely dubious. Historically two of the main popular political forces – Communism and Shi'ite radical Islamism – are basically hostile to the West; the third, Kurdish nationalism, is a problematic partner because of its potential to destabilize other states with Kurdish minorities – most importantly from Washington's point of view, Turkey. There is no real counterpart to the very substantial sections of the old Stalinist *nomenklatura* in Eastern and Central Europe and the former Soviet Union that provided the social base for the transition in these countries to market capitalism, reinventing themselves as liberal-democratic politicians and/or private entrepreneurs – apart, that is, for the remnants of the old Ba'athist ruling party. One of the most striking developments after the fall of Saddam was the demonstration by the Shi'ites – 60 per cent of Iraq's population – of formidable powers of self-organization. The prospect of an Iraqi version of the Shi'ite Islamic republic in Iran did not please the

Bush administration. 'A regime like that in Iran is not compatible with our vision of Iraq,' said US Defense Secretary Donald Rumsfeld.[39] The freedom brought to the people of Iraq by American arms apparently does not embrace the right to support political forces of which Washington disapproves.

The favour that the Pentagon has shown as shopworn a figure as Ahmad Chalabi therefore makes a certain amount of sense. Scion of a family close to the Hashemite monarchy that was overthrown in the Iraqi Revolution of 1958, Chalabi had to flee Jordan in 1989 (according to some stories, in the boot of a car) after the Jordanian government seized his Petra Bank. He was subsequently sentenced in absentia to twenty-two years of hard labour for embezzlement and other crimes: an auditors' report estimated that the bank's assets had been overstated by $200 million. This setback didn't prevent Chalabi from establishing the Iraqi National Congress in 1992, with considerable support from the CIA. Eventually the intelligence agencies and the State Department grew weary of his failure to mobilize significant resistance on the ground and cut off the INC's funding. But the contacts he had cultivated with the Republican right – including such key figures as Paul Wolfowitz and Richard Perle – ensured that, under Bush, the cause of Chalabi and the INC has been strongly promoted by the Defense Department.[40] Precisely because Chalabi has no domestic base to speak of he is unlikely to pursue policies that significantly threaten the interests of his American patrons – though after the invasion the INC soon found itself forced publicly to distance itself from the US occupation authorities in the hope of winning popular support within Iraq.

The apparent contradiction involved in seeking to impose democracy on a society in the absence of domestic forces capable of sustaining it – at least in a form compatible with US interests – may be dissolved or at least alleviated once we consider what is understood by 'democracy' here. Bush's preface to the main programmatic document of his administration, *The National Security Strategy of the United States of America*, begins by affirming: 'The great struggles of the twentieth century between liberty and totalitarianism ended with a decisive victory for the forces of freedom – and a single sustainable model for national success: freedom, democracy, and free enterprise.' Bush goes on to avow the intention 'to create a balance of power that favours human freedom: conditions in which all nations and societies can choose for themselves the rewards and challenges of political and economic liberty.'[41]

It is clear that by the 'single sustainable model for national success' Bush means American-style free-market capitalism, and that, consequently, democracy here has a significant *economic* content. This is confirmed by the rest of the *National Security Strategy*. An entire chapter is devoted to outlining neoliberal policies that will 'Ignite a New Era of Global Growth through Free Markets and Free Trade'. This includes the following splendidly Thatcherite homily: 'The concept of "free trade" arose as a moral principle even before it became a pillar of economics. If you can make something that others value, you should be able to sell it to them. If others make something that you value, you should be able to buy it. This is real freedom, the freedom for a person – or a nation – to make a living.'[42]

Elsewhere the document criticizes Russia for its 'uneven commitment to the basic values of free-market democracy' and predicts that China 'will find that social and political freedom is the only source of that greatness'. The document also notes: 'The US national security strategy will be based on a distinctly American internationalism that reflects the union of our values and our national success.' It is indeed a peculiar kind of internationalism that leaves peoples free to choose the 'single sustainable model of national success' – American-style laissez-faire capitalism. A new era of Great Power competition can thus be avoided so long as potential challengers such as Russia and China not only renounce any challenge to US hegemony but also sign up to 'common values', which means, of course, American liberal capitalist values.[43]

Once we recognize the centrality of free-market capitalism to the conception of democracy espoused by the Bush administration, we can see that a displacement in the understanding of democracy itself is going on. Democracy is *par excellence* an essentially contested concept, but it is undeniable that one of its main strands is the active participation by citizens in the processes through which they are governed.[44] But in the version of democracy that ideologically supports the Bush administration's global strategy this element is marginalized. One interesting example of this process is provided by a policy intellectual deeply implicated in the Democratic wing of the American establishment, Philip Bobbitt. In his vast – and vastly overpraised – book *The Shield of Achilles* Bobbitt argues that 'we are witnessing the emergence of the *market-state* and the shift to that form from the constitutional order of the nation-state that has dominated the twentieth century.' The critical difference between these two forms is that the nation-state 'took responsibility for the well-being of groups', while the market-state is concerned with 'maximizing the choices available to individuals. This means lowering the transaction costs of choosing by individuals and that often means restraining rather than empowering governments.'[45]

Plainly Bobbitt has in mind the political and economic changes involved in the shift over the past generation from Keynesian economic policies to the currently dominant neoliberal agenda of deregulation, privatization and market liberalization. But he spells out what he sees as a political implication of this transformation in a remarkable passage that merits quotation at length:

the market-state does not suffer from the acute shame experienced by the nation-state when the subject of campaign finance comes up. When Chief Justice Earl Warren wrote that 'Congressmen do not represent interests or trees, they represent people,' he was expressing an axiom of the nation-state. Doubtless he believed it, but it would be hard to maintain this view in the light of today's functional patronage of candidates by contributors . . . The market-state is not so squeamish. Indeed its civic lessons hold that there should be no limits on campaign spending from any source so that the true opportunity cost of a campaign's defeat are reflected in the probability of his victory. The market-state merely tries to get the 'best' person for the job in the way that universities try to get the 'best' students: they set up a market that selects persons on the basis of predictions about their subsequent success . . . Governance becomes a matter of maintaining popularity, which requires further advertising, which requires further fund-raising. The candidate who is tied to important interests by virtue of his fund-raising is precisely the person whose vote will most closely reflect those interests. The more money he raises, the more attractive the candidacy, because successful fund-raising reflects the relationship between the importance of the interests he represents and his ability to represent them (as those interests judge it – and who are better placed to do so than they?). And this is just as well, because initiatives, plebiscites, and referenda are, like elections, very expensive. The more frequently they come, the greater the match between economic interests and public policy; indeed, this is one of the attractions of the market-state. That this change places enormous power in the hands of the media only underscores the change in its constitutional role with the emergence of the market-state.[46]

There is no doubt that Bobbitt paints an accurate picture of American democracy in the era of Clinton and the younger Bush. A good example of 'functional patronage' is provided by the current US Vice President, Dick Cheney, who still receives 'deferred compensation' worth up to $1 million a year from Halliburton, the oil company that he used to head and that was one of the six big American corporations invited secretly to bid for work to reconstruct Iraq; its subsidiary Kellogg, Brown & Root was awarded a contract possibly worth $7 billion to put out oil well fires and also, it later emerged, actually to operate oilfields in Iraq.[47] But Bobbitt goes beyond mere description, and in a clumsily reasoned kind of vulgar Hegelianism argues that this isn't just how things are, but is (just because it is) how things should be. In the 'constitutional order' of the market-state, the interests that count are those that can mobilize the money to buy candidates and elections, and it is right that they should shape the political process. This is a revealing insight into the assumptions shared by the American policy elite, whether Republican or Democratic.

Against this background there is no necessary contradiction between the promises to bring democracy to Iraq and the American occupation authorities' intention, in Rumsfeld's words, that 'market-run systems will be favoured . . . The coalition will encourage moves to privatize state-owned enterprises.'[48] Philip Mattera wrote during the early days of the war on Iraq in March 2003:

> An explicit call for privatization . . . was issued last fall at a conference convened by the right-wing Heritage Foundation. In a paper presented at that conference (and revised last month) Ariel Cohen and Gerald O'Driscoll wrote: 'to rehabilitate and modernize its economy, a post-Saddam government will need to move simultaneously on a number of economic policy fronts, utilizing the experience of privatization campaigns and structural reforms in other countries.' The authors go on to assert what they call Lesson No. 1: 'Privatization Works Everywhere'. . . As with other Iraq matters, the US calls for privatization have been echoed in Britain. Last month, the free-market loving Adam Smith Institute issued a paper titled 'Toward an Economic and Governance Agenda for a New Iraq'. One section of the document starts out with the declaration: 'Privatization is a sine qua non for successful reform in Iraq.' The authors go on to say: 'In Iraq there is much to privatize, as a considerable portion of the economy is state-

owned.' Among the sectors up for grabs, they suggest, are mining, chemicals and construction.[49]

Mattera notes that Bechtel Corp, lead bidder for the contract to reconstruct Iraq, 'is a leading player in water system privatization, ranking just behind the big three – Suez, Vivendi Universal and RWE/Thames Water – in that controversial business'. But the greatest prize in Iraq is, of course, as we shall discuss further in chapter 4 below, the country's oil reserves, the second largest in the world. Washington's intentions were indicated by the appointment of Philip Carroll, former chief executive officer of Shell, to supervise the Iraqi oil industry. After the United Nations Security Council decided in May 2003 to legitimize the Anglo-American occupation of Iraq and transfer control of the country's oil to Washington and London, the *Financial Times* reported: 'Countries from all over the world have been clamouring for a piece of the work.' Briefings organized by Bechtel for potential subcontractors attracted 1,800 companies in Washington and over 1,000 in London.[50] Paul Bremer, the neoconservative ex-diplomat appointed by Rumsfeld as chief of the 'Coalition Provisional Authority' in Iraq promised to move the country in a 'clear direction towards a liberal, market-run economy'; meanwhile the Iraqi Oil Ministry cancelled production contracts signed with Russian and Chinese companies under Saddam.[51]

From the perspective developed by Bobbitt, it is simply naive to condemn this process as looting. A private enterprise economy organized along the lines laid down by the neoliberal Washington Consensus just is an essential constituent of democracy – of what the *National Security Strategy* calls 'real freedom'. Arundhati Roy puts it well: 'Democracy has become Empire's euphemism for neoliberal capitalism.'[52] And if Iraq's most productive assets end up owned by foreign corporations – well, isn't that the case in most of the rest of the world? Of course, economic liberalization and privatization aren't quite enough to constitute 'democratic governance'. After suitable pummelling and manipulation, some selection of Iraq's elites will no doubt be proclaimed an 'interim administration', just as Hamid Karzai was groomed to become president of Afghanistan after the fall of the Taliban. This is not, however, a particularly prepossessing precedent, since Karzai's writ hardly runs beyond the boundaries of Kabul (and his personal security is in the hands of a praetorian guard of American mercenaries); elsewhere the warlords who tore Afghanistan apart before the Taliban seized control are back in power. But even if a stronger post-Saddam regime emerges in Iraq thanks to American patronage, many will find it hard to distinguish this kind of democracy-lite from older forms of colonialism.

Liberal alibis

Of course, the 'war on terrorism', and even the conquest of Iraq found support on the left as well as the Republican right. Indeed, the 11 September attacks were the occasion of one well-publicized apostasy, as Christopher Hitchens, hitherto a trenchant critic of American foreign policy, rallied round the flag.[53] But prowar intellectuals who claimed a left-wing allegiance had little distinctive to say. The philosopher Michael Walzer is perhaps best known for writing a book called *Just and Unjust Wars*. After 9/11, when the clarity and detachment in which philosophers are supposed to specialize was especially needed, Walzer simply echoed the rantings of the Republican right. He denounced 'a culture of excuse and apology' and opposed any changes in US Middle East policy, even if justified on other grounds, in case they could 'be construed as appeasement'.[54] He later wondered whether America could have a 'decent left', where the criterion of decency appeared to be supporting the United States in its wars.[55]

Confronted with a war in Iraq that he had opposed beforehand, Walzer engaged in a positive frenzy of casuistry in order to remain true to the standard he had set himself. 'America's war is unjust,' he explained, but then so too was Saddam's. Forced to choose between these two injustices, Walzer opted for Uncle Sam: 'now that we are fighting it, I hope that we win it and that the Iraqi regime collapses quickly. I will not march to stop the war now while Saddam is still standing, for that would strengthen his tyranny at home and make him, once again, a threat to his neighbours.' But, puzzlingly, Walzer's real ire was reserved for France, Germany and Russia, who had opposed a war that he had also been against. 'We were committed, too soon, to war; they were committed, all along, to appeasement.'[56] Walzer and Hitchens sometimes seek to demonstrate their left-wing credentials by invoking the names of great socialist internationalists like Rosa Luxemburg and Karl Liebknecht. But Walzer seems intent on inverting Liebknecht's famous slogan, coined during the First World War: for Walzer, the main enemy is always abroad.

Given the poverty of such 'philosophical' thinking, it is not particularly surprising that the most coherent argument that the centre-left should support the 'war on terrorism' came from the politician who, George Bush aside, is most closely identified with it – Tony Blair. Already during the Kosovo war in 1999 he had advanced the most ambitious justification for the Western powers overriding Yugoslav sovereignty. He argued that globalization was a multidimensional process – economic, political, security, cultural – that required the formulation of a new 'doctrine of international community' under which it was legitimate to intervene in states that violated generally accepted democratic norms.[57] Community is indeed the master concept of Blair's ideology of the Third Way: it is by virtue of the integrative powers of community that, as he put it, 'enterprise and justice can live together' – in other words, that neoliberal economics and the traditional social-democratic commitment to equality can be reconciled.[58]

Blair brought these different themes together in his most celebrated response to 9/11, the speech he made to the Labour Party conference on 2 October 2001. Though the speech had a directly political function – to rally Labour activists already nervous about the likely American response to the attacks on New York and Washington behind the war that would begin in Afghanistan five days later, Blair used it to offer the closest that there has come to a left-wing case for backing Bush. Unlike Walzer, he was willing implicitly to acknowledge that the causes of terrorism have to be addressed. Indeed, to adapt the slogan that first made Blair famous, the entire thrust of the speech might be described as 'tough on terrorism, tough on the causes of terrorism'. He surveyed the global condition, invoking various ills – Africa ('a scar on the conscience of the world'), global warming, the conflicts in Israel/Palestine and in the north of Ireland – and addressed the movement against capitalist globalization that only a few months earlier in July 2001 had mounted a spectacular challenge to the G8 summit in Genoa:

> I realize why people protest against globalization. We watch aspects of it with trepidation. We feel powerless, as if we were now pushed to and fro by forces beyond our control. But there's a risk that political leaders, faced with street demonstrations, pander to the argument rather than answer it. The demonstrators are right to say that there's injustice, poverty, environmental degradation. But globalization is a fact and, by and large, it is driven by people . . . And in trade, the problem is not that there's too much of it; on the contrary, there's too little of it. The issue is not how to stop globalization. The issue is how we use the power of community to combine it with justice. If globalization works only for the few, then it will fail and deserve to fail. But if we follow the principles that have served us so well at home – that power, wealth, opportunity must be in the hands of the many, not the few – if we make that the guiding light for the global economy, then it will be a force for good and an international movement that we should take pride in leading.[59]

So the answer to al-Qaeda was, on the one hand, daisy-cutter bombs and, on the other, a global version of the Third Way. Blair returned to this theme in his peroration:

> So I believe this is a fight for freedom. And I want to make it a fight for justice too. Justice not only to punish the guilty. But justice to bring those same values of democracy and freedom to people round the world. And I mean: freedom, not only in the narrow sense of personal liberty but in the broader sense of each individual having the economic and social freedom to develop their potential to the full. That is what community means, founded on the equal worth of all. The starving, the wretched, the dispossessed, the ignorant, those living in want and squalor from the deserts of Northern Africa to the slums of Gaza, to the mountain ranges of Afghanistan: they too are our cause. This is a moment to seize. The Kaleidoscope has been shaken. The pieces are in flux. Soon they will settle again. Before they do, let us re-order this world around us.[60]

On the face of it, this was the most extraordinary imperialist arrogance, asserting the right of the 'international community' – i.e. the Western powers with the US and Britain at their core – to 're-order the world'. But Blair was offering more than just democracy-lite: he was promising social justice – 'each individual having the economic and social freedom to develop their potential to the full'. Achieving *that* really would be reordering the world. But seriously pursuing the egalitarian justice he evoked in this speech is just what Blair cannot do. This is for two reasons. The first has to do with the internal contradictions of the ideology of the Third Way. Blair, as I have already said, was offering a global version of what he sought in Britain: a reordered international community that could reconcile 'enterprise and justice'. But the word 'enterprise' highlights the problem. Blair argued that the further extension of the global market ('in trade, the problem is not that there's too much of it; on the contrary, there's too little of it') would allow 'power, wealth, and opportunity' to spread from 'the few' to 'the many'. But the experience of the past quarter century, when neoliberal economics have come increasingly to dominate policy-making worldwide, points in precisely the opposite direction. Freeing up markets hasn't spread power and advantage from the many to the few, but has rather directed them more narrowly towards a small minority of the world's population. There is no harmonious community in which 'enterprise and justice can live together', but rather a world riven by harsh inequalities and conflicts of interest.[61]

But secondly, even if Blair's solution were theoretically feasible, how could it be achieved in partnership with the administration of George W. Bush? Liberal critics of the Republican right in the US have characterized the latter's domestic ambition as being nothing less than to wipe away the social and economic consequences of the entire twentieth century. Targeted in particular are the social programmes put into place by two Democratic presidents – Franklin Roosevelt's New Deal in the 1930s and Lyndon Johnson's Great Society in the 1960s – and the accompanying shift of power away from local and state governments to Washington. Many American conservatives want to turn the clock back to an idealized version of the social relationships that prevailed around 1900, when William McKinley was President and no progressive income tax existed to transfer resources from rich to poor. They want Big Government to be dismantled, and private enterprise to flourish unfettered by any state-imposed requirement to help the less successful. There are widespread suspicions that the Bush administration's insistence on pressing ahead with massive tax cuts despite the spectacular growth in the federal budget deficit is motivated by the desire to engineer a deficit crisis that will make it easier to force through drastic cuts in public expenditure – except, of course, in the sacrosanct sphere of defence.[62]

It doesn't matter for our purposes whether or not the right's ideal society is more than a reactionary Utopia. The crucial point is this: is an administration that subscribes to it as a desirable goal for the US going readily to endorse the kind of redistributive measures required to reduce global economy inequality – for example, the Global Resources Dividend offered as a 'moderate proposal' by Thomas Pogge for addressing what he calls radical inequality?[63] One has only to pose the question to answer it: it isn't going to happen. The younger Bush's administration has pursued the neoliberal economic agenda it inherited from its predecessors – for example, pressing for the new round of trade liberalization talks that were launched by the World Trade Organization summit in Doha in November 2001. Where the administration has deviated from this agenda, it has been in the direction of the unilateral assertion of US economic interests – for example, the imposition of tariffs on imported steel and the introduction of increased agricultural subsidies. These interests were, of course, also invoked by Bush when he denounced the Kyoto protocol on global warming. Free-market conservatism with a dash of protectionism and plenty of military Keynesianism: this is hardly a recipe for pursuing global economic justice.

This leaves Tony Blair exactly in the place that he currently occupies in international politics – as the eloquent and earnest English lawyer of an American government that holds the rest of the world largely in contempt.[64] They certainly want to reorder the world, but not for the sake of the wretched of the earth. Liberal-left defenders of the 'war on terrorism' are thus reduced to repeating the dubious arguments I have reviewed in the earlier parts of this chapter. One of them, Michael Ignatieff, writes: 'Yet it remains a fact – as disagreeable to those left wingers who regard American imperialism as the root of all evil as it is to right-wing isolationists – that there are many peoples who owe their freedom to an exercise of American military power.'[65] And indeed American arms did overthrow Saddam Hussein's thoroughly evil regime. But all this does is remind us of the long-familiar moral fact that a wicked act – in this case, a war of aggression – can have some good consequences. This does not extinguish the evil consequences it has also brought, either directly – in the case of the war on Iraq, not simply the death, suffering and destruction it caused, but the country's political and economic subordination to the United States – or indirectly – the precedent offered by the American conquest of Iraq for 'preventive' wars launched against vulnerable states deemed to be a threat by the aggressor. Nor does it imply that we should support future wars of the same type: in an era of pre-emptive wars evil would easily and completely overwhelm good. It is, more than anything else, this prospect that brought tens of millions of people onto the streets to protest against the war on Iraq in the early months of 2003.

Perhaps the most honest expression of the outlook of the prowar centre-left is provided by Robert Cooper, a British diplomat and adviser to Tony Blair. He distinguishes between the 'postmodern world', notably in Europe, that 'represents security through transparency, and transparency through interdependence', on the one hand, and the 'modern world' of competing nation-states and 'premodern world . . . of failed states' that still survive elsewhere, on the other hand:

> The challenge to the postmodern world is to get used to double standards. Among ourselves, we operate on the basis of laws and open cooperative security. But when dealing with old-fashioned kinds of states outside the postmodern continent of Europe, we need to revert to the rougher methods of an earlier era – force, pre-emptive attack, deception, whatever is necessary to deal with those who still live in the nineteenth century world of 'every state for itself'. Among ourselves, we keep the law but when we are operating in the jungle, we must also use the laws of the jungle.[66]

Cooper proposes 'a new kind of imperialism, one acceptable to a world of human rights and cosmopolitan values'.[67] In fact, however, his argument resonates with the outlook of Victorian imperialism, where one set of standards applied to the 'civilized' insiders and another to the 'barbarous' outsiders. Daniel Bensaïd suggests, however, that that, alongside the hypocrisies familiar from the age of classical colonialism, is something more disturbing. 'The commanders of humanitarian war in fact arrogate for themselves the exorbitant right to trace a new frontier between the human and the inhuman. The enemy then loses his quality of enemy to fall under the disquieting category of the monster. There is a short step from the symbolic bestialization of the enemy to his practical animalization', as Camp X-Ray at Guantanomo Bay and Israel's practice of 'extra-judicial executions' of Palestinian activists show.[68] If Bush and Blair are really looking for monsters, they have only to look in the mirror.

– 2 –

The Cultists of Eternal War

The Bush Doctrine

Even George W. Bush's 'axis of evil' speech did not fully reveal the scale of his administration's ambitions. These only became clear when he announced what the *Financial Times* called 'an entirely fresh doctrine of pre-emptive action' in a speech at West Point on 1 June 2002.[1] Bush said:

> For much of the past century, America's defense relied on the Cold War doctrines of deterrence and containment. In some cases, those strategies still apply. But new threats also require new thinking. Deterrence – the promise of massive retaliation against nations – means nothing against shadowy terrorist networks with no nation or citizens to defend. Containment is not possible when unbalanced dictators with weapons of mass destruction can deliver those weapons on missiles or secretly provide them to terrorist allies.
>
> We cannot defend America and our friends by hoping for the best. We cannot put our faith in the word of tyrants, who solemnly sign non-proliferation treaties, and then systematically break them. If we wait for threats to fully materialize, we will have waited too long. (Applause.)

Homeland defense and missile defense are part of stronger security, and they're essential priorities for America. But the war on terror will not be won on the defensive. We must take the battle to the enemy, disrupt his plans, and confront the worst threats before they emerge. (Applause.) In the world we have entered, the only path to safety is the path of action. And this nation will act. (Applause.)[2]

This Bush Doctrine of (as one administration official put it) 'pre-emptive retaliation' is enshrined in the *National Security Strategy*: 'While the United States will constantly strive to enlist the support of the international community, we will not hesitate to act alone, if necessary, to exercise our right of self-defense by acting pre-emptively.'[3] It is important to put this in some historical perspective. Central to the strategy of the United States throughout the Cold War was a policy of containing the USSR – that is, America should resist any attempts to extend the bloc that had been carved out by Soviet arms in Central and Eastern Europe during the latter phases of the Second World War rather than take offensive action to dismantle this rival empire. This was the strategy – what its architect George Kennan called 'a long-term, patient but firm and vigilant containment of Russian expansive tendencies' through 'the adroit and vigilant application of counter-force at a series of shifting geographical and political points, corresponding to the shifts and manoeuvres of Soviet policy' – first outlined in Kennan's famous 'Long Telegram' of February 1946 and pursued by both Democratic and Republican administrations subsequently.[4]

Containment survived the collapse of the Soviet Union. US policy in the Middle East after the 1991 Gulf War was one of what was called 'dual containment', designed to isolate both Iran and Iraq. In the case of Iraq, a combination of economic sanctions and bombing raids was intended to keep the Ba'athist regime of Saddam Hussein weak and on the defensive. By the late 1990s the policy was falling apart diplomatically, since permanent Security

Council members such as France and Russia and the Arab states were showing an increasing interest in strengthening their economic and diplomatic links with Iraq. To maintain the isolation of Iraq, the US and Britain were forced increasingly to take unilateral action, in particular through an intensified bombing campaign.[5] As recently as 2000, Condoleezza Rice (then a Stanford professor advising the Bush campaign) was arguing for a continuation of this policy. Referring to 'rogue states' such as Iraq and North Korea, she wrote:

> These regimes are living on borrowed time, so there need be no sense of panic about them. Rather, the first line of defense should be a clear and classical statement of deterrence – if they do acquire WMD [weapons of mass destruction] – their weapons will be unusable because any attempt to use them will bring national obliteration.[6]

Challenged about these remarks after the unveiling of the Bush Doctrine, Rice, now National Security Advisor, joked feebly that 'academics can write anything', and appealed to the awful warning of 9/11.[7] The argument is hardly persuasive. Nothing that has happened since the attacks on the US has altered the fact that any state that mounted a nuclear, chemical, or biological strike against America would be committing national suicide.[8] To understand the Bush Doctrine we need, to start with, to take a closer look at the Bush administration itself.

Bush II: the Republican right take the helm

The administration of the younger Bush tended initially to be presented as a continuation of his father's. The same view is expressed in the commonplace claim that the war on Iraq was a settling of an old family score. Interpretations of this kind are fundamentally mistaken.[9] Though much of the top personnel of the present administration served under George H. W. Bush between 1989 and 1993, ideologically Bush II harks back to the era of Ronald Reagan, president during the last phase of the Cold War between 1981 and 1989. It was Reagan who denounced the Soviet Union as an 'evil empire' and authorized the CIA and the Pentagon to back right-wing guerrilla movements against Third World nationalist regimes such as those in Nicaragua and Angola that the US deemed to be on the wrong side in the Cold War.[10] The arch-cynic Henry Kissinger admiringly summed up Reagan's foreign policy thus: 'The high-flying Wilsonian language in support of freedom and democracy was leavened by almost Machiavellian realism ... the Reagan Doctrine amounted to a strategy for helping the enemy of one's enemy – of which Richelieu would have approved.'[11] (One of the beneficiaries of this strategy proved to be Osama bin Laden.)

Bush *fils* has clearly modelled his personal style on that of Reagan – the folksy great communicator who concentrated on getting (from the perspective of the Republican right) the big issues right. More importantly, the central axis of his administration is defined by the politics of Reaganism. The elder Bush was a product of the East Coast establishment: the tone of his foreign policy was set by his Secretary of State, James Baker, who carefully constructed a broad coalition based on the authority of the UN Security Council to wage the 1991 war against Iraq, unlike the ersatz affair confected to conquer the country twelve years later. Baker also withheld a $10 billion US loan guarantee to Israel to force the right-wing prime minister, Yitzhak Shamir, to take part in the Madrid peace conference with the Palestine Liberation Organization.[12]

Dick Cheney, the younger Bush's highly influential Vice President, was a relatively isolated figure when he served as Defense Secretary under Bush *père*. In March 1992 a draft Pentagon *Defense Planning Guidance* document was leaked to the *New York Times*:

> Our first objective is to prevent the re-emergence of a new rival. This is a dominant consideration underlying the new

regional defense strategy and requires that we endeavour to prevent any hostile power from dominating a region whose resources would, under consolidated control, be sufficient to generate global power.

There are three additional aspects to this objective. First, the US must show the leadership necessary to establish and protect a new order that holds the promise of convincing potential competitors that they need not aspire to a greater role or pursue a more aggressive posture to protect their legitimate interests. Second, in the non-defense areas, we must account sufficiently for the interests of the advanced industrial nations to discourage them from challenging our leadership or seeking to overturn the established political and economic order. Finally, we must maintain the mechanisms for deterring competitors from even aspiring to a larger regional or global role.[13]

This document, which was repudiated by the administration of the elder Bush, anticipated the global strategy pursued by the US under his son. It was drafted under the supervision of Paul Wolfowitz, today Deputy Defense Secretary under Donald Rumsfeld. In the administration of Gerald Ford (1974–7), Rumsfeld served as the President's Chief of Staff and then as Secretary of Defense. His successor as White House Chief of Staff was his friend and protégé Dick Cheney. Kissinger, Secretary of State in the same administration, ruefully described Rumsfeld – whose obstruction blocked his efforts to conclude the SALT II treaty with the USSR limiting nuclear arsenals – as an example of 'the special Washington phenomenon, the skilled full-time politician-bureaucrat in whom ambition, ability, and substance fuse seamlessly'.[14] Bob Woodward reports that there was a 'subtle rivalry' between Rumsfeld and the elder Bush dating back to their time serving together as young Republican Congressmen in the 1960s. Apparently Rumsfeld regarded Bush as a 'lightweight' who lacked 'clear goals' and who was, under Ford, a 'weak CIA director who seriously underestimated the Soviet Union's military advances'.[15] During the Clinton administration

Rumsfeld chaired a congressional commission that recommended that the US develop a National Missile Defense system.

Under the younger Bush, Cheney, Rumsfeld and Wolfowitz form the core of a group of right-wing Republican intellectuals that is setting the administration's global agenda. Others include Condoleezza Rice at the National Security Council, John Bolton, Under Secretary of State for Arms Control and International Affairs, Douglas Feith, Under Secretary of Defense for Policy, and Richard Perle, baptized the 'prince of darkness' for his role in the Pentagon under Reagan and chairman of the advisory Defense Policy Board under Bush Junior until he was forced in March 2003 to resign over alleged conflicts of interest (he had been retained by Global Crossing to help overcome the Pentagon's veto of the proposed sale of the bankrupt telecom company's assets to a Chinese-controlled firm). As Frances Fitzgerald puts it, 'what had been a minority position in the first Bush administration had become a majority position in the second.'[16] It was Secretary of State Colin Powell, as Chairman of the Joint Chiefs of Staff under Bush Senior the architect of the 1991 Gulf War, who found himself isolated when he argued for a response to 9/11 that put the emphasis on building a broad international coalition against al-Qaeda.

Michael Lind, who himself once frequented right-wing Republican circles as executive editor of the neoconservative journal *The National Interest*, has provided a vivid portrait of the right-wing camarilla at the heart of the Bush administration.

Most neo-conservative defense intellectuals have their roots on the left, not the right. They are products of the largely Jewish-American Trotskyist movement of the 1930s and 1940s, which morphed into anti-communist liberalism between the 1950s and the 1970s and finally into a kind of militarist and imperial right with no precedents in American culture or political history.[17]

Lind is here confusing an earlier generation of neoconservative intellectuals, some of whom did originate in the Trotskyist movement, with those currently in the saddle in Washington.[18] Unless we count the recent arrival Christopher Hitchens, no prominent figure on the contemporary Republican right has a Trotskyist background. A much more significant intellectual influence would seem to be the political philosopher Leo Strauss, who taught at the University of Chicago, where many neoconservative intellectuals were students. Wolfowitz studied under Strauss in 1972, as did Abram Shulsky, director of the Office of Special Plans at the Pentagon, which has been accused of constructing a case for invading Iraq based on dubious evidence provided by defectors and the Iraqi National Congress. Strauss was a conservative critic of modernity and a sceptic about democracy who conceived philosophy as an esoteric wisdom to be concealed from the vulgar masses. He seems to have endorsed the view he attributed to Xenophon: 'The best regime is then an aristocracy disguised as democracy.'[19] One can see how such an outlook would be congenial to a clique (the Straussians at the Office of Special Plans call themselves 'the Cabal') intent on manipulating public opinion in support of their imperial designs.[20]

Chronicle of a war foretold

We shall look more closely at the administration's global strategy in the next chapter. For the moment it is worth documenting how the right-wing Republican core of the Bush team built up a case for war in the Middle East long before 9/11. One crucial dimension in this campaign is the close links that have developed between American neoconservatives and the Israeli right. This is a significant historical shift: if anything, Republican administrations tended on the whole to be more wary of Israel than their

Democratic counterparts. Richard Nixon assured four embarrassed Arab oil ministers in October 1973 that they could trust his Secretary of State: 'A Jewish-American can be a good American, and Henry Kissinger is a good American.'[21] Today, by contrast, close links exist between leading neoconservatives and the Israeli political elite – Perle, for example, is a director of the *Jerusalem Post*, who sought to use his influence in Israel in a clumsy attempt to sabotage the Camp David peace talks in 2000. Christian fundamentalists – an indispensable element in Bush's political base – also have incorporated support for Israel into their millenarian worldview: they see Palestine as the land given by God to the Jews in the Old Testament and regard the return of the world's Jews to a triumphant Israel as a precondition of the Second Coming.

A consequence is a close identification by many Republican right-wingers of the strategic interests of Israel with those of the United States, as well as the hostility towards the Middle East peace process that they share with Likud leaders such as Ariel Sharon and Binyamin Netanyahu. Thus in 1996 Perle, Feith and, among others, David Wurmser (now a senior adviser to John Bolton at the State Department) co-authored a document for Netanyahu, then freshly elected Prime Minister, calling for Israel to 'work closely with Turkey and Jordan to contain, destabilize and roll back some of its most dangerous threats. This implies a clean break from the slogan "comprehensive peace" to a traditional concept of strategy based on balance of power.' Chief among these threats were Syria and Iraq. The document argues: 'Israel can shape its environment, in cooperation with Turkey and Jordan, by weakening, containing, and even rolling back Syria. This effort can focus on removing Saddam Hussein from power in Iraq – an important Israeli strategic objective in its own right – as a means of foiling Syria's regional ambitions.' In conclusion, 'Israel's new agenda can signal a clean break by abandoning a policy which assumed exhaustion and allowed strategic retreat by re-establishing the principle of pre-emption, rather than retaliation alone and by ceasing to absorb blows to the nation without response.'[22]

Though the analysis here is couched in terms of Israel's strategic predicament, for the Republic right the same diagnosis applied also to the United States. In 1997 William Kristol, editor of *The Weekly Standard*, a neoconservative magazine owned by Rupert Murdoch, launched the Project for the New American Century. Its founding statement bewailed what it condemned as the neglectful policies of the Clinton administration:

> We are living off the capital – both the military investments and the foreign policy achievements – built up by past administrations . . . We seem to have forgotten the essential elements of the Reagan administration's success: a military that is strong and ready to meet both present and future challenges; a foreign policy that boldly and purposefully promotes American principles abroad; and national leadership that accepts the United States's global responsibilities.[23]

As in the earlier proposals for a 'clean break' in Israeli strategy, this call for a return to 'a Reaganite policy of military strength and moral clarity' was closely linked in the mind of the Republican right to the overthrow of Saddam Hussein. In January 1998 the Project for the New American Century sponsored a letter to Clinton denouncing the failure of the policy of containing Iraq and declaring: 'The only acceptable strategy is one that eliminates the possibility that Iraq will be able to use or to threaten to use weapons of mass destruction. In the near term, this means a willingness to undertake military action as diplomacy is clearly failing. In the long term, it means removing Saddam Hussein and his regime from power.' The signatories read like a roll call of the Bush administration that would take office three years later. They included Richard Armitage, John Bolton, Zalmay Khalilzad, Richard Perle, Donald Rumsfeld, Paul Wolfowitz and Robert Zoellick.[24] This

campaign, along with Chalabi's lobbying, helped to per-
suade the Republican-dominated US Congress to pass in
October 1998 the Iraq Liberation Act, which allocated
$97 million to arm and train the Iraqi opposition. *The
Weekly Standard* carried a special issue in December 1998
headlined 'Saddam Must Go: A How-To Guide' that
carried articles by Wolfowitz and Khalilzad, later Bush's
emissary to Afghanistan and to the Iraqi opposition.
Regime change in Iraq was thus embraced by the
Republican right as a political objective long before 9/11.
Its leading figures were quick to seize the opportunity provided by the attacks on Washington and New York. On
11 September itself, sitting in a Pentagon still smoking
from the impact of the hijacked airliner that had been
flown into it, Rumsfeld scribbled a note: 'Judge whether
good enough hit SH [Saddam Hussein] at the same time.
Not only UBL [bin Laden].'[25] He asked at a National Security Council meeting the morning after: 'Why shouldn't we
go against Iraq, not just al-Qaeda?' The next day Wolfowitz gave a press briefing in which he implicitly connected the 'war on terrorism' to attacking Iraq: 'It's not
just simply a matter of capturing people and holding them
accountable, but removing the sanctuaries, removing the
support systems, ending states who sponsor terrorism.' At
the first serious planning meeting of Bush and his 'princi-
pals' at Camp David on 15 September Wolfowitz pressed
the case for an attack on Iraq, though Powell resisted such
a move because it would split the anti-terrorist coalition.
Bush's response was initially non-committal.[26] A 'senior
Administration official' told Nicholas Lemann:

> Before September 11th, there wasn't a consensus Admin-
> istration view about Iraq. This issue hadn't come to the
> fore, and you had Administration *views* ... Then, in the
> immediate aftermath of the eleventh, not that much
> changed. The focus was on Afghanistan, Osama bin
> Laden, al-Qaeda. Some initial attempts by Wolfowitz and
> others to draw Iraq in never went anywhere, because the

link between Iraq and September 11th was, as far as we
know, nebulous at most – nonexistent for all intents and
purposes. It's somewhere in the first half of 2002 that all
this changed. The President internalized the idea of making
regime change a priority.[27]

According to a *Washington Post* investigation, Bush
directed the Pentagon to draft plans for an invasion of Iraq
as early as 17 September 2001, though the decision to go
to war was only taken in the following spring. 'By the time
the policy was set, opponents were left arguing over tactics
– such as whether to go to the United Nations – without
clearly understanding how the decision was reached in the
first place. "It simply snuck up on us," a senior State
Department official said.'[28] When Richard Haass, Director
of the Policy Planning Staff at the State Department, asked
Condoleezza Rice whether 'we wanted to put Iraq front
and centre at this point' at a meeting in early July 2002,
'she said, essentially, that the decision's been made, don't
waste your breath.'[29] If the decision was taken around
March 2002, this was, of course, months before the US
went to the United Nations Security Council and secured
Resolution 1441 that reinstated weapons inspection in
Iraq on a much tougher basis than the regime instituted at
the end of the 1991 Gulf War.

More than this, the decision to go to war cannot seriously be conceived as a response to 9/11. Not only did
the campaign for regime change precede the attacks on the
US, but, as the official quoted above admitted, the 'link
between Iraq and 11th September was . . . nonexistent for
all intents and purposes.' Moreover, once Baghdad had
fallen, Saddam's fabled weapons of mass destruction
turned out to be just that – creatures of fable. Some advocates of war on Iraq had been quite open in affirming that
WMD weren't the real issue. George Friedman of the
private intelligence analysis company Stratfor criticized the
Bush administration for having 'allowed the WMD issue
to supplant US strategic interests as the justification for

war', and declared that 'invading Iraq is in the US national interest regardless of whether Hussein has a single weapon of mass destruction.'[30]

After the conquest of Iraq, 'a senior Bush administration official' admitted to the *Financial Times* that 'he would be "amazed if we found weapons-grade plutonium or uranium" and that it was unlikely large volumes of biological or chemical material would be discovered.'[31] Rumsfeld publicly conceded: 'It is also possible that they [the Saddam regime] decided that they would destroy them [the WMD] prior to a conflict.'[32] None of this stopped Bush blithely asserting: 'We've removed an ally of al-Qaeda and cut off a source of terrorist funding. And this much is certain: No terrorist networks will gain weapons of mass destruction from this regime, because the regime is no more.'[33] As Goebbels said, the big lies are the best. For those not content with official propaganda and its media amplifications, the real question is this: what is it about 'US strategic interests', at least as the Republican right defines them, that made, not just war on Iraq, but the wider strategy based on the assertion of American military power so imperative?

– 3 –

The Grand Strategy of the American Empire

American strategy after the Cold War

The Bush administration's global strategy scares a lot of people, including many who would normally support the role of the United States as the lynchpin of the Western system of alliances. Anatole Lieven of the Carnegie Endowment for International Peace writes that 'the generally agreed plan is unilateral world domination through absolute military superiority.'[1] It would, however, be a mistake to see this doctrine as simply a triumphalist assertion of American military supremacy. The Washington neoconservatives' outlook is more complex, as James Fallows puts it, 'defined by pessimism, optimism, and impatience with procedure'.[2] Properly to understand this mixture we need to set it in a more long-term historical context. There are important discontinuities between US global policy under the younger Bush and that of his predecessors, but there are also continuities. Unilateralism did not spring out fully formed once the Republicans reoccupied the White House in January 2001. Moreover, the US has fought no fewer than four major wars since the end of the Cold War: the Gulf (1991) under the elder Bush,

Yugoslavia (1999) under Clinton, Afghanistan (2001) and Iraq (2003), both under the younger Bush. This is now too long a series of military conflicts to be dismissed merely as a cumulation of accidents, let alone as simply the work of wild ideologues in Washington. What are the larger patterns involved here? Edward Luttwak, a brilliant but idiosyncratic American conservative, defines grand strategy as the dimension of interstate conflict 'where all that is military happens within the much broader context of domestic politics, international diplomacy, economic activity, and all else that strengthens and weakens'.[3] So what is the grand strategy of the American empire under George W. Bush?

The proper starting point for answering this question is 1945.[4] Indeed, well before the defeat of Germany and Japan, US planners were drafting a strategy for the postwar world. First, they sought a unified world economy based on free trade that would give American companies the kind of unfettered access to markets and investments that had been denied them thanks to the spread of protectionism during the Great Depression of the 1930s. Harking back to Woodrow Wilson's proposals for reconstructing the global order after the First World War, this 'liberal grand strategy' (as John Ikenberry calls it) postulated a direct connection between the economic prosperity that free trade was supposed to produce and the spread of liberal-democratic political institutions that would increasingly render interstate wars obsolete. Multilateral bodies such as the United Nations and the International Monetary Fund would provide the framework in which this liberal world order could develop. Second, Pentagon planners sought two objectives – maintaining American military predominance in the Western Hemisphere and ensuring that no hostile power or coalition of powers emerged in the Eurasian landmass.

Developments in the second half of the 1940s compromised this project. On the one hand, the Soviet Union and its client states resisted inclusion in a liberal capitalist world system that would compromise the state control of the economy that was a crucial lynchpin of *nomenklatura* power. On the other hand, economic collapse and political instability in Western and Southern Europe seemed to threaten to tip the strategic balance towards Moscow, a process that a declining Britain was unable to reverse. This prompted a triple response on the part of the United States under the Truman presidency (1945–53) that set the pattern of global politics for the next forty years. First, US rearmament and the construction of a series of American-led military alliances sought to contain the USSR and its allies. Secondly, a programme of economic aid (in Europe the Marshall Plan) combined with political initiatives from Washington served in particular to rehabilitate West Germany and Japan as significant powers (albeit reconstructed as liberal capitalist states and incorporated into the US alliance system) that could help counteract Soviet influence. Thirdly, though the international state system was now polarized between two rival military and ideological blocs, the multilateral institutions set up in the immediate postwar period served to unify the Western camp into a version of the liberal global order envisaged by American planners, albeit modified to accommodate the strong pressures from Washington's European allies and indeed domestic political forces for Keynesian demand management and relatively generous welfare states.

The formation of American global strategy during the Second World War offers a useful historical perspective on the very different conjuncture we face at the beginning of the twenty-first century. For one thing this perspective draws attention to the deep historical roots of what Tony Smith calls 'national security liberalism', whose

> chief proposition . . . is that self-interest – the enhancement of American influence in the world – and the morally correct thing to do – a foreign policy supporting human rights and the establishment of democratic governments abroad – may actually serve one another far more often

and importantly than many commentators on the US role in world affairs generally suppose.[5]

From a rather less uncritical standpoint Andrew Bacevich argues that 'since the end of the Cold War the United States has pursued a well-defined grand strategy' that in its essentials has been followed by every American administration since the start of the twentieth century. Its aim

is to preserve and, where both feasible and conducive to US interests, to expand an American imperium. Central to this strategy is a commitment to global openness – removing barriers that inhibit the movement of goods, capital, ideas, and people. Its ultimate objective is the creation of an integrated international order based on the principles of democratic capitalism, with the United States as the ultimate guarantor of order and enforcer of norms.[6]

Precisely this connection between US global interests and the promotion of liberal capitalism is made by the neoconservatives currently directing American foreign policy. The phrase used by both George W. Bush and Condoleezza Rice of 'a balance of power that favours freedom' nicely captures the fusion of ideology and realpolitik involved. Similarly, Lawrence Kaplan and William Kristol argue that the younger Bush's 'distinctly American internationalism' implies a 'national security strategy [that] seeks to minimize the gap between ideals and interests, between morality and power', and invoke the Truman, Kennedy and Reagan administrations as models for the synthesis of realism and liberalism embodied in this strategy.[7]

Reviewing the world after the end of the Cold War, Henry Kissinger defined US strategic interests in precisely the same terms as those used by American planners on the eve of that conflict:

Geopolitically, America is an island off the shores of the large landmass of Eurasia, whose resources and population far exceed those of the United States. The domination by a single power of either of Eurasia's two principal spheres – Europe or Asia – remains a good definition of strategic danger for America, Cold War or no Cold War. For such a grouping would have the capacity to outstrip America economically and, in the end, militarily.[8]

The revolutions in East and Central Europe in 1989 and the collapse of the Soviet Union in 1991 left the US as the leading military power. It also gave American capitalism access to regions previously closed off to it by the Cold War partition of the world into rival superpower blocs, most notably Central Asia, both a site of important energy reserves and strategically placed at the boundary between Russian and Chinese spheres of influence. Nevertheless, the disintegration of the Stalinist system did not abolish rivalries among the Great Powers. Kissinger indeed argued:

> Victory in the Cold War has propelled America into a world which bears many similarities to the European state system of the eighteenth and nineteenth centuries, and to practices which American statesmen and thinkers have consistently questioned. The absence of both an overriding ideological or strategic threat frees nations to pursue foreign policies based increasingly on their immediate interest. In an international system characterized by perhaps five or six major powers and a multiplicity of smaller states, order will have to emerge as it did in past centuries from a reconciliation and balancing of competing national interests.[9]

In the event, the administrations of both Clinton and the younger Bush renounced open reliance on the kind of balance-of-power politics that Kissinger had practised as first National Security Advisor and then Secretary of State under the Nixon and Ford administrations (1969–77). Nevertheless the premiss of his argument was true: now that the relative discipline imposed by the bipolar structure of international politics during the Cold War had been removed, the world was entering a period of intensified geopolitical competition and therefore of greater instability and danger than had prevailed before 1989.[10] More specifically, American hegemony faced two potential sources of challenge. The first came from within the Western bloc. Germany and Japan had been firmly subordinated to US political and military leadership throughout the Cold War, but they had developed into major economic rivals to American capitalism. Consequent US relative economic decline was one of the main driving forces behind the world economy's entry into a new era of crises at the end of the 1960s.[11] Liberated from the restraints demanded by unity against the Eastern bloc, Germany and Japan might increasingly assert themselves geopolitically and develop into world powers threatening US hegemony. Though it was a newly reunified Germany that flaunted its independence of Washington (for example, by helping to engineer the disintegration of Yugoslavia in 1991–2 in defiance of the efforts by the administration of the elder Bush to keep the federation together), Japan's penetration of US markets and its growing investments in the American homeland made it seem the greater threat. George Friedman of the private intelligence analysis company Stratfor even co-authored a book in the early 1990s that announced *The Coming War with Japan*.

The second group of potential rivals came from outside the Western bloc. Russia, though impoverished and descending into social and political chaos, remained a Great Power, armed with thousands of nuclear warheads, sprawling across Eurasia, encompassing or bordering on vast energy reserves. More threatening still was China. The rapid economic growth that China has clocked up since its rulers embraced market Stalinism in the 1980s might seem to vindicate laissez-faire capitalism, but it also gave them the resources with which to build up China as a major military power in the most geopolitically unstable region in the world.[12] Indeed, as the Japanese economic challenge receded in the course of the 1990s, China loomed ever larger in the minds of American policy-makers as the major long-term threat facing them. One leading international relations specialist, John Mearsheimer, wrote recently:

> Another way of illustrating how powerful China might become if its economy continues growing rapidly is to compare it with the United States. The GNP of the United States is $7.9 trillion. If China's per capita GNP equals [South] Korea's, China's overall GNP would be almost $10.66 trillion, which is about 1.35 times the size of America's GNP. If China's per capita GNP is half of Japan's, China's overall GNP would then be roughly 2.5 times bigger than America's. For purposes of comparison, the Soviet Union was roughly one-half as wealthy as the United States during most of the Cold War . . . China, in short, has the potential to be considerably more powerful than even the United States.[13]

On the basis of this projection, Mearsheimer goes on to construct a grim scenario for North East Asia and indeed the world:

> Not only would China be much wealthier than any of its Asian rivals . . . but its huge population advantage would allow it to build a far more powerful army than either Japan or Russia could. China would also have the resources to acquire an impressive nuclear arsenal. Northeast Asia . . . would be a far more dangerous place than it is now. China, like all previous potential hegemons, would be strongly inclined to become a real hegemon, and all its rivals, including the United States, would encircle China to try to keep it from expanding.[14]

Others such as Zbigniew Brzezinski are much more sceptical about China's capacity to develop into a serious challenger to US hegemony, particularly when predictions involve (as Mearsheimer's arguably do) 'the mechanical reliance on statistical projections'.[15] All the same,

Brzezinski has been among the most forceful to argue that the challenge facing the American ruling class since the end of the Cold War has been to preserve its leadership of the Western capitalist states and to extend it to incorporate the other Great Powers. The main geopolitical success of the Clinton administration (1993–2001) was that it succeeded in maintaining a reorganized US hegemony in Eurasia. This was greatly facilitated by the economic background. For most of the 1990s, the American economy enjoyed a boom that grew in strength in the course of the decade.[16] Meanwhile, the German economy stagnated for much of that decade, while Japan suffered the most serious deflationary slump experienced by any major capitalist state since the 1930s. This relative shift in the balance of economic power in favour of the US was reinforced by the Clinton administration's selective use of its military might. The Nato bombing campaigns against Serbia over Bosnia in 1995 and – on a much greater scale – over Kosovo in 1999 served to underline the dependence of the European Union on American political leadership and military muscle to overcome crises even in its own backyard in the Balkans. Bacevich coldly cuts through the afflatus of liberal humanitarianism used to justify Nato's 1999 intervention in Yugoslavia:

> the intent of Operation Allied Force was to provide an object lesson to any European state fancying that it was exempt from the rules of the post-Cold War era. It was not Kosovo that counted, but affirming the dominant position of the United States in a Europe that was unified, integrated, and open.[17]

The expansion of Nato into East and Central Europe which took effect during the 1999 Balkan War performed a triple function: (1) it both maintained the position of the US, established during the Cold War, as the leading power in Western Europe and extended it eastwards; (2) it legitimized the penetration of the economically and strategically crucial zone of Central Asia by a US-led Nato now authorized to undertake 'out-of-area' operations; (3) it amounted to a new strategy of encirclement directed towards a Russia that US policy-makers had concluded was unlikely somehow to metamorphose into a prosperous liberal democracy and would therefore have to be contained.[18] The first test of the new Nato against Serbia was at best equivocal in its results, since the bombing campaign (which caused little serious damage to the Yugoslav army though much to the country's civilian infrastructure) was only one of the factors that prompted Slobodan Milošević to abandon Kosovo: Russian refusal to back him and pressure to strike a deal probably played at least as important a role. But the Balkan War was the occasion on which the ideology of humanitarian intervention was most forcefully invoked, particularly by Tony Blair, in order to assert the right of the 'international community' – in this case the US and its European allies – to override national sovereignty and wage war ostensibly at least to punish violations of human rights by 'rogue states'.[19]

On the face of it, then, the Clinton administration pursued a multilateralist strategy. The real motives behind this strategy were, however, much more clearly exposed by Brzezinski, who was one of the main architects of Nato expansion. In *The Grand Chessboard* (1997) he presented this policy as one facet of a much broader approach to maintain American dominance over Eurasia through a continent-wide policy of divide and rule. Brzezinski openly used the language of imperial power:

America's global supremacy is reminiscent in some ways of earlier empires, notwithstanding their more confined regional scope. These empires based their power on a hierarchy of vassals, tributaries, protectorates, and colonies, with those on the outside generally viewed as barbarians. To some degree, this anachronistic terminology is not inappropriate for some of the states currently within the American orbit.[20]

Like Kissinger, Brzezinski argued that 'America's global primacy is directly dependent on how long and how effectively its preponderance on the Eurasian continent is sustained.' To secure this objective he advocated US coalition-building in order 'to offset, co-opt, and/or control' potential rivals such as Germany, Russia, China, and Japan:

> *In the short run, it is in America's interest to consolidate and perpetuate the prevailing geographical pluralism on the map of Eurasia.* *That puts a premium on maneuver and manipulation in order to prevent the emergence of a hostile coalition that would eventually seek to challenge America's primacy, not to mention the remote possibility of any one particular state seeking to do so.* By the middle term [the next twenty years or so], *the foregoing should gradually yield to a greater emphasis on the emergence of increasingly important but strategically compatible partners who, prompted by American leadership, might help to shape a more cooperative trans-Eurasian security system. Eventually, in the much longer run still, the foregoing could phase into a global core of genuinely shared political responsibility.*[21]

It is important to understand, however, that despite this emphasis on coalition-building (and Brzezinksi's willingness to envisage some genuinely cooperative relationship among the Great Powers in the very remote future), the Clinton administration's strategy was not in any simple sense a multilateralist one. Promoting the expansion of Nato and the EU was a means of maintaining American hegemony in Eurasia, not an alternative to US primacy. Clinton and his advisers were what Robert Kagan calls 'instrumental multilateralists': 'Americans prefer to act with the sanction and support of other countries if they can. But they're strong enough to act alone if they must.'[22] The US initiated the 1999 Balkan War under the aegis of Nato, without reference to the United Nations Security Council. The Clinton administration had already flouted the UN when it launched a bombing campaign against Iraq in December 1998 with the support of Britain and Kuwait. Madeleine Albright, the peculiarly inept and arrogant Secretary of State during Clinton's second term, justified an earlier cruise missile attack on Iraq by saying: 'If we have to use force, it is because we are America. We are the indispensable nation. We stand tall. We see farther into the future.'[23] Bacevich argues that Albright effectively abandoned the post-Vietnam military doctrine devised in the 1980s by Reagan's Defense Secretary, Caspar Weinberger, and reaffirmed by Colin Powell as Chairman of the Joint Chiefs of Staff – essentially 'a belief in overwhelming force employed decisively on behalf of vital interests'. In the Balkans and Western Asia, the Clinton administration gradually shifted towards 'expending American military power for limited and carefully (indeed, often publicly) delineated purposes while avoiding the prospect of resembling "combat"'. As a result, Bacevich notes, 'US foreign policy became increasingly militarized.'[24]

Exploiting America's military edge

Despite the drift towards unilateralism and the use of carefully dosed applications of force under Clinton, George W. Bush has presided over a radicalization of this approach that amounts to a rejection of Brzezinski's strategy of coalition-building as a means of maintaining American primacy. The administration's attitude to Nato is symptomatic of the shift involved. On 12 September 2001, the North Atlantic Council invoked, for the first time in its history, Article 5 of the 1949 treaty establishing Nato and declared that the attacks on the US were attacks on all the alliance's member states. Bush pocketed this declaration of solidarity along with a UN Security Council resolution, but the Pentagon didn't bother to use Nato in its war against Afghanistan. Nato, which barely two years before had been Washington's preferred instrument of intervention in the Balkans, was now treated with the same contempt that had become habitual in American dealings with the UN. The *National Security Strategy* devotes a mere three paragraphs to it. In February 2003, Nato was thrown into even deeper crisis when France, Germany and Belgium blocked the use of alliance military assets to protect Turkey in the event of it being used for the Anglo-American attack on Iraq; subsequently in Turkey itself popular pressure forced the government to refuse the US and Britain access to its territory.

The Bush administration's preference for unilateral military action supported by what Donald Rumsfeld calls 'coalitions of the willing' reflected in the first instance the serious symbolic blow that American power had suffered on 11 September. After the spectacular attacks on its financial capital and military headquarters, the American state had to be seen to be striking back itself, not dialling 911 for the international police. The American 'homeland' had been violated: American power had to be seen taking revenge. Pentagon chiefs had in any case made clear their impatience with Nato's cumbersome procedures during the 1999 Balkan War. But, after the fall of Kabul in November 2001, it became clear that the Bush administration was using the 'war on terrorism' to justify a much more aggressive geopolitical strategy deploying military power to eliminate some threats and intimidate everyone else.

At its roots, this strategy is not a response to the 11 September attacks. In a revealing passage, Rice put it like this:

> an earthquake of the magnitude of 9/11 can shift the tectonic plates of international politics. The international system has been in flux since the collapse of Soviet power. Now it is possible – indeed, probable – that that transition is coming to an end.
>
> If that is right, if the collapse of the Soviet Union and 9/11 bookend a major shift in international politics, then this is a period not just of grave danger, but of enormous opportunity. Before the clay is dry again, America and our friends and allies must move to take advantage of these

new opportunities. This is, then, a period akin to 1945 to 1947, when American leadership expanded the number of free and democratic states – Japan and Germany among the great powers – to create a balance of power that favoured freedom.[25]

Rice said 'she had called together the senior staff people of the National Security Council and asked them to think seriously about "how do you capitalize on these opportunities" to fundamentally change American doctrine, and the shape of the world after September 11th.'[26] So 9/11 wasn't just a disaster but an opportunity to 'shift the tectonic plates of international politics' in the way that the Truman administration did in the late 1940s. According to Bob Woodward, 'Rice admired what Truman and his secretaries of state had done after World War II. The Truman Doctrine, the Marshall Plan and the policy of containment were smart, effective uses of political capital.'[27] The Truman Doctrine, proclaimed to a joint session of Congress on 12 March 1947, responded to a national crisis – the Greek civil war – with the declaration: 'it must be the policy of the United States to support free peoples who are resisting attempted subjugation by armed minorities or by outside pressures.' One of Truman's Secretaries of State, Dean Acheson, famously admitted later that 'we made our points clearer than truth', hyping up Communism as a worldwide threat to freedom in order to win domestic political support for American rearmament and aid to Europe.[28] His biographer James Chace comments: 'By using universalistic rhetoric to attain more modest ends, Acheson and Truman laid the groundwork for the belief . . . that the United States saw little alternative but to embark on the global containment of communism.'[29]

The arguments behind the Bush Doctrine – developed in a series of dramatic addresses often to joint sessions of Congress – are similarly being put in a way 'clearer than truth'. (Indeed it is striking how the neoconservatives' vocabulary is full of terms – 'containment', 'deterrence', 'preventive war', 'rollback' – that date back to American strategic debates during the Cold War.)[30] The Republican right's concern is not confined to Islamist terrorism or the 'rogue states' that may (or more typically may not) sustain it. The pessimism that, as I have already suggested, is an important element in their outlook is chiefly represented by the belief that America's present supremacy may soon be challenged by the emergence of new peer competitors. This assessment was strikingly expressed by Paul Wolfowitz in an essay he wrote under Clinton. He compared the post-1989 triumphalism about the victory of liberal capitalism and the End of History to the view widely held at the end of the nineteenth century that economic growth and international integration had made war obsolete:

> The end of this century resembles the end of the last in another important way, one that puts a question mark over the great hopes for continued peace and prosperity as we enter the twenty-first century. Alongside the remarkable and peaceful progress that was taking place at the end of the last century, the world was grappling with – or, more accurately, failing to manage – the emergence of major new powers. Not only was Japan newly powerful in Asia, but Germany, which had not even existed before the end of the nineteenth century, was becoming a dominant force in Europe.
>
> Today, the same spectacular economic growth that is reducing poverty, expanding trade, and creating new middle classes is also creating new economic powers and possibly new military ones as well. This is particularly true in Asia . . . The emergence of China by itself would present sizable problems; the emergence of China along with a number of other Asian powers presents an extremely complicated equation. In the case of China, there is the obvious element of its outsider status. To hark back to the last turning of a century, the obvious and disturbing analogy is [with] the position of Germany, a country that felt it had been denied its 'place in the sun', that believed it had been

mistreated by the other powers, and that was determined to achieve its rightful place by nationalistic assertiveness.[31]

It is this world-historical vision that informs the Bush team's preoccupation with asserting American military power in order to block the emergence of challengers. Their thinking is well expressed in a report written by Zalmay Khalilzad for a military think-tank, the RAND Corporation's Project AIR FORCE, in the mid-1990s. Khalilzad's career offers a small insight into the world of the Republican right. Originating in the Afghan royal court that was removed from power by a military coup in 1973, he studied at the University of Chicago, one of the nurseries of American neoconservatism, and went on to work in the State Department under Reagan (where he was a strong advocate of arming the Afghan mujahedin against the Soviet occupation forces) and as one of Dick Cheney's Assistant Under Secretaries of Defense under the elder Bush. During the Clinton years, apart from working at RAND, he advised the oil company Unocal, which in the mid-1990s led a consortium seeking to develop a gas pipeline from Turkmenistan through Afghanistan and Pakistan. It was presumably as part of Unocal's efforts to court the Taliban then in control of Afghanistan that in 1997 Khalilzad wrote an article in the *Washington Post* arguing that the US should 'reengage' with Afghanistan and denying that the Taliban represented 'the kind of anti-US style of fundamentalism practised by Iran'. Appointed Special Assistant to the President for Near East, Southwest Asian and North African Affairs by the younger Bush, Khalilzad took on the task of special US envoy to Afghanistan after the overthrow of the Taliban with no apparent signs of discomfort, and later performed the same role with the Iraqi opponents of Saddam Hussein.[32]

In his 1995 report Khalilzad lamented the absence of a US grand strategy after the Cold War and reviewed three possible candidates for the role. The first, a retreat into isolationism, risked 'establishing a favourable climate for the spread of disorder – in other words, a return to conditions similar to those of the first half of the twentieth century'. The second strategy, a version of that advocated by Kissinger, would see the US trying 'to mimic the former British role of an offshore "balancer" ', intervening to prevent the emergence of hegemonic powers or coalitions in Europe or Asia in a multipolar world. Among the disadvantages of this approach were the development of economically destabilizing conflicts among the liberal capitalist states, the danger that other powers might not respect the American sphere of influence in the Western Hemisphere, and the risk that the US would prove no more successful than Britain ultimately was in preventing Great Power rivalries developing into a general war. Khalilzad concluded that the third strategy, 'US global leadership and deterring the rise of another hostile global rival or a return to multipolarity for the indefinite future is the best long-term guiding principle and vision.' Under US leadership, 'the global environment will be more open and more receptive to American values', 'such a world has a better chance of dealing cooperatively with its major problems', and it would be easier 'to preclude the rise of another hostile global rival'. This somewhat circular reasoning indicates the importance of this last objective to Khalilzad, who elaborated thus:

> A global rival could emerge if a hostile power or coalition gained hegemony over a critical region. Therefore it is a vital US interest to preclude such a development – i.e. to be willing to use force if necessary for the purpose. A region can be defined as critical if it contains sufficient economic, technical, and human resources so that a hostile power that gained control over it could pose a global challenge. Although this could change in the future, two regions now meet this criterion: East Asia and Europe. The Persian Gulf is very important for a different reason – its oil resources are vital for the world economy.[33]

The basic objectives implicit in Khalilzad's argument – preserving American predominance in the Western Hemisphere and primacy in Eurasia – does not set it apart from mainstream US strategic thinking. But what is more distinctive is the preoccupation with the rise of a potential challenger to American hegemony and the emphasis on a resort to force as the ultimate response (not that Brzezinski or Kissinger, for example, would be at all squeamish about the use of military power, as their records indicate, but they would be less likely to highlight it). In these respects, Khalilzad's analysis is representative of neoconservative thinking more broadly. Towards the end of the Clinton presidency, a commission (including Wolfowitz among a *galère* of Republican ideologues) that was set up by the Project for the New American Century to review US defence strategy complained that 'the 1990s have been "a decade of defense neglect"' and warned:

> At present the United States faces no global rival. America's grand strategy should aim to preserve and extend this advantageous position as far into the future as possible. There are, however, potentially powerful states dissatisfied with the current situation and eager to change, if they can, in directions that endanger the relatively peaceful, prosperous and free condition the world enjoys today. Up to now, they have been deterred by the capability and global presence of American military power. But, as that power declines, relatively and absolutely, the happy conditions that follow from it will inevitably be undermined.[34]

It is this world-historical perspective that has led the Bush team to conclude that a window of opportunity has opened in which they can use America's present military superiority to maintain and perhaps even extend US global hegemony. The events of 11 September and the 'war on terrorism' have provided the occasion for this effort, but the US is after much bigger game than the elusive bin Laden and his al-Qaeda network or petty tyrants such as Saddam Hussein or Kim Jong-Il. A key section of the *National Security Strategy* warns: 'We are attentive to the possible renewal of old patterns of great power competition. Several potential great powers are now in the midst of internal transition – most importantly Russia, India, and China.' While insisting that these powers share common interests and values with the US, the document directs a very specific warning at Beijing:

> a quarter century after beginning the process of shedding the worst features of the Communist legacy, China's leaders have not yet made the next series of fundamental choices about the character of the state. In pursuing advanced military capabilities that can threaten its neighbours in the Asia-Pacific region, China is pursuing an outdated path that, in the end, will hamper its own pursuit of national greatness. In time, China will find that social and political freedom is the only source of that greatness.[35]

In other words, the consensus that Bush and his advisers are seeking among the Great Powers is one on American terms. Only the US is allowed to develop 'advanced military capabilities'. The *National Security Strategy* begins with the affirmation: 'The United States possesses unprecedented – and unequalled – strength and influence in the world', and concludes with the warning: 'Our forces will be strong enough to dissuade potential adversaries from pursuing a military build-up in the hopes of surpassing, or equalling, the power of the United States.'[36] In the same vein, the Project for the New American Century's commission on defence strategy affirmed:

> what should finally drive the size and character of our nuclear forces is not numerical parity with Russian capabilities but maintaining American strategic superiority – and with that superiority, a capability to deter possible hostile coalitions of nuclear powers. US nuclear superiority is nothing to be ashamed of; rather, it will be an essential element in preserving American leadership in a more complex and chaotic world.[37]

In the light of such statements it is hardly surprising that Russia and China should fear that the scrapping of the

Anti-Ballistic Missile Treaty and the construction of the National Missile Defense system by the Bush administration are designed to give the US a nuclear first-strike capability that would perpetuate American supremacy. Leading neoconservatives have indeed said as much. 'Missile defense isn't really meant to defend America,' explained Lawrence Kaplan. 'It's a tool for global dominance.'[38] The administration's Nuclear Posture Review, leaked in early 2002, listed Russia, China, North Korea, Iran, Iraq, Syria and Libya as potential nuclear adversaries and proposed the integration of nuclear and conventional capabilities – for example, the addition of nuclear warheads to bunker buster weapons intended to kill enemy leaders.[39]

Meanwhile, the 'war on terrorism' provided the US with an opportunity to establish a string of military bases in Central Asia – a region closed to it during the Cold War – and to return its troops to the Philippines, where American bases had been abandoned in the early 1990s. The *National Security Strategy* emphasizes that this is no temporary development: 'To contend with uncertainty and to meet the many security challenges we face, the United States will require bases and stations within and beyond Western Europe and Northeast Asia, as well as temporary access arrangements for the long-distance deployment of US forces.'[40] No one could blame China's rulers if they saw these moves as the first stage in a strategy of encirclement directed at them.

The effect is of these moves to accelerate a process that, as we have seen, was already under way under Clinton, namely the militarization of US global policy. Dana Priest of the *Washington Post* writes:

> Long before September 11, the US government had come increasingly dependent on its military to carry out its foreign affairs. The shift was incremental, little noticed, de facto. It did not even qualify as an 'approach'. The military simply filled a vacuum left by an indecisive White

House, an atrophied State Department, and a distracted Congress. After September 11, however, the trend accelerated dramatically with the war in Afghanistan and the likelihood of US military operations elsewhere. Without a doubt, US-sponsored political reform is being eclipsed by new military pacts focusing on anti-terrorism and intelligence gathering.[41]

In her fascinating study of the contemporary American military, Priest stresses the importance of the five regional 'unified combatant commands'. She writes of the commanders-in-chief of the four commands covering the world outside the continental US:

> the CinCs grew into a powerful force in US foreign policy because of the disproportionate weight of their resources and organization in relation to the assets and influence of other parts of America's foreign policy structure – in particular, the State Department, which was shrivelling in size, stature, and spirit even as the military's role expanded.[42]

The chiefs of the regional commands have by law direct access to the Secretary of Defense and the President. The combined annual budget for their headquarters (which includes a long-distance aircraft for each CinC to tour his domain) is $380 million. Southern Command HQ, which covers Latin America, has a staff of 1,100: 'More people work there dealing with Latin American matters than at the departments of State, Commerce, Treasury, and Agriculture, the Pentagon's Joint Staff and the office of the secretary of defense combined.' Pacific Command has headquarters staff numbering 3,600, and Central Command – covering the strategically crucial regions of Western and Central Asia – 1,100. CinC European Command is also Supreme Allied Commander, Europe, presiding over Nato's military forces. General Anthony Zinni, who preceded Tommy Franks (the military architect of the Bush administration's wars in Afghanistan and

Iraq) as CinC Central Command, said 'he had become a modern-day proconsul, descendant of the warrior-statesmen who ruled the Roman Empire's outlying territory, bringing order and ideals from a legalistic Rome.'[43]

It is instructive to reflect that the ascension of an imperial American military took place during the 1990s, at exactly the time when enthusiasts for globalization were announcing an end to war and interstate rivalries. This development helps to explain why the present drive to maintain American hegemony, though informed by a sense of potential long-term weakness, is also undergirded by confidence. In part this derives from the outcome of the Cold War. As Fallows puts it,

> the confidence lies in the conviction that if the United States confronts 'evil' enemies, it can win. The proof is, of course, the Soviet Union's fall. Ronald Reagan came to office calling not for détente but for outright victory over the 'evil empire'. Ten years later the empire was gone. Nearly all the members of today's defense leadership were part of Reagan's team. The memory of that success lies behind George W. Bush's promise that terrorists will be not just contained, like drug traffickers, but beaten, like Nazis and Soviets.[44]

But this confidence is reinforced by the successes the US military have enjoyed in the post-Cold War era, and in particular by the role of air power in securing victory against Iraq in 1991, Yugoslavia in 1999, Afghanistan in 2001 and Iraq again in 2003.[45] Before 11 September Rumsfeld was struggling to force through a transformation of the American military against the resistance of the Pentagon. This involved using the so-called 'Revolution in Military Affairs' made possible in particular by the development of information technology to reorganize the US armed forces into relatively small specialized units supported by a variety of forms of air power employing precision guided munitions. In a key speech in January 2002, Rumsfeld compared the assault on Mazar-e-Sharif by the Northern

Alliance and US Special Forces during the Afghan War of
2001 to the Nazi blitzkrieg in 1939–41:

> What was revolutionary and unprecedented about the
> blitzkrieg was not the new capabilities the Germans
> employed, but rather the revolutionary and unprecedented
> ways in which they mixed new and existing capabilities.
> In a similar way, the battle for Mazar was a transfor-
> mational battle. Coalition forces took existing military
> capabilities – from the most advanced (such as laser-guided
> weapons) to the antique (40-year-old B-52s updated with
> modern electronics) to the most rudimentary (a man on a
> horse with a weapon) – and used them together in unpre-
> cedented ways, with devastating effect on enemy positions,
> on enemy morale – and, this time, the cause of evil in the
> world.[46]

The victorious American drive to Baghdad also approxi-
mated to Rumsfeld's conception of 'transformational
warfare', in part because he slimmed down the Pentagon's
plans for a huge mechanized force including at least four
army divisions, in part because US commanders were
forced to improvise after the Turkish parliament refused
to allow the 4th Infantry Division to invade northern Iraq
from their territory.[47] At the beginning of the Iraq War,
Edward Luttwak wrote that the US was conducting 'a
high-risk campaign of psychological warfare, whose enormously ambitious aim is to wholly detach the Iraqi armed
forces – Republican Guards included – from Saddam's
regime, so they will not resist US and British forces at all.'[48]
Though the Anglo-American invasion initially ran into
heavier than expected resistance and failed to provoke the
uprisings that Washington's Iraqi protégés had promised,
its ultimate success depended on a version of the tactics
described by Luttwak: a forced march on Baghdad that
maximized America's overwhelming superiority in air
power and mechanized warfare to attack the symbols of
Ba'athist power and thereby to precipitate the regime's
collapse (though these tactics also left the comparatively

small invasion army relatively ill-prepared for the chaos that ensued).

'Shock and Awe' was the phrase used by the Pentagon and its media claque to characterize this campaign. It was coined by the American military academic Harlan Ullman: 'The basis for rapid dominance rests in the ability to affect the will, perception, and understanding through imposing sufficient shock and awe to achieve the necessary political, strategic and operational goals of the conflict or crisis that led to the use of force.' Among the examples of this approach Ullman includes the nuclear bombing of Hiroshima and Nagasaki and the Nazi blitzkrieg.[49] We should see 'Shock and Awe' as being directed today much more broadly than at the immediate enemy. The destruction of the Saddam Hussein regime served as a demonstration to all other states in the world of the costs of defying American power.

America versus Europe

Confidence in US military supremacy certainly informs what Fallows describes as the Washington neoconservatives' 'impatience with procedure'. In the first place, they are even less willing than their Republican or Democratic predecessors to pay lip-service to international institutions. John Bolton accurately summed up this attitude when he said: 'There is no such thing as the United Nations. There is an international community that can be led by the only real power left in the world, and that is the United States, when it suits our interests and when we can get others to go along.'[50] As the US and Britain went to war against Iraq without the sanction of the UN Security Council, Richard Perle announced the death of 'the fantasy of the UN as the foundation for a new world order' amid 'the intellectual wreckage of the liberal conceit of safety through international law administered by international institutions'.[51]

This stance represents a shift in emphasis rather than a break with the past: as we have already seen, the Clinton administration was ready enough to bypass the UN and take unilateral action when it deemed it necessary. But the younger Bush's administration is much more open in the disdain it expresses, not merely for international institutions, but also for the other leading liberal capitalist states in Western Europe and East Asia. It quickly ran into a series of conflicts with the European Union over the Kyoto protocol, trade (in particular the US imposition of steel tariffs), and American opposition to the International Criminal Court. The underlying contempt and even outright hostility felt by the Republican right for the Europeans were very effectively evoked by Anatol Lieven in the immediate aftermath of 9/11:

> Not long after the Bush administration took power in January, I was invited to lunch at a glamorous restaurant in New York by a group of editors and writers from an influential American right-wing broadsheet. The food and wine were extremely expensive, the décor luxurious but discreet, the clientele beautifully dressed, and much of the conversation more than mildly insane. With regard to the greater part of the world outside America, my hosts' attitude was a combination of loathing, contempt, distrust and fear: not only towards Arabs, Russians, Chinese, French and others, but towards 'European socialist governments', whatever that was supposed to mean. This went with a strong desire – in theory at least – to take military action against a broad range of countries across the world.

Lieven quotes a leading Republican politician who asked: 'Who says we share common values with the Europeans? They don't even go to church.'[52]

Robert Kagan, Lieven's colleague at the Carnegie Endowment for International Peace, has developed a somewhat more sophisticated neoconservative analysis, according to which the American preference for unilateralism and the European commitment to multilateralism flow from 'the power gap' between the two sides:

> Strong powers naturally view the world differently than weak powers . . . Those with great military power are more likely to consider force a useful tool of international relations than those who have less military power . . . Europe's relative weakness has produced a perfectly understandable aversion to the exercise of military power. Indeed, it has produced a powerful European interest in inhabiting a world where strength doesn't matter, where international law and international institutions predominate, where unilateral action by powerful actions is forbidden, where all nations regardless of their strength have equal rights and are equally protected by commonly agreed-upon international rules of behaviour. Europeans have a deep interest in devaluing and eventually eradicating the brutal laws of an anarchic, Hobbesian world where power is the ultimate determinant of national security and success.[53]

Kagan argues that these consequences of the differences in material power between the US and Europe were reinforced by the development through the process of European integration of multilateral institutions encouraging the reconciliation of national interests. But the taming of interstate rivalries within Europe depended on the American military umbrella:

> By providing security from outside, the United States has rendered it unnecessary for Europe's supranational government to provide it . . . The current situation abounds in ironies. Europe's rejection of power politics and its devaluing of military force as a tool of international relations have depended on the presence of American military forces on European soil. Europe's new Kantian order could flourish only under the umbrella of American power exercised according to the rules of the old Hobbesian order. American power made it possible for Europeans to believe that power was no longer important.[54]

On the basis of this thesis Kagan criticizes the idea, put forward by Francis Fukuyama and followers such as Robert Cooper, that, with the End of History, advanced capitalism has entered a 'postmodern', 'posthistorical' era in which war is obsolete within this bloc, even though it may still be a threat in the 'modern' or even 'premodern' parts of the world.[55] *Europe* may indeed have gone beyond history, Kagan argues, but

> although the United States has played the critical role in bringing Europe into this Kantian paradise, and still plays a key role in making that paradise possible, it cannot enter this paradise itself. It mans the walls but cannot walk through the gate. The United States, with all its vast power, remains stuck in history, left to deal with the Saddams and the ayatollahs, the Kim Jong-Ils and the Jiang Zemins, leaving most of the benefits to others.[56]

This self-image of the US as a sentry selflessly shouldering the military burden required to keep Europeans gambolling in a postmodern paradise would naturally breed resentment. The underlying tensions burst to the surface in the debates over the war in Iraq that pitted the US and Britain against France, Germany and Russia, when American Congressmen and British tabloids campaigned to have French fries renamed 'freedom fries'. Such infantilisms aside, the real significance of this split requires separate assessment. But we must first consider a final element in the Republican right's global strategy – their plans to remake the Middle East.

– 4 –

The Geopolitics of Oil

Remaking the Middle East

The geostrategy pursued by the Bush team has in its sights the major rivals of the United States. But the first major step they took was forcibly to remove Saddam Hussein. This enterprise served two main functions. First, in terms of the broader strategy, the conquest of Iraq would be an example *pour encourager les autres*: if overwhelming US force can remove the recalcitrant ruler of a minor Middle Eastern power, then Washington's potential peer competitors had better watch their step. Secondly, bringing down Saddam was intended to play a more specific role in an ambitious programme that at least some on the Republican right harbour for reordering the entire Middle East.

High on the neoconservatives' list of targets is Saudi Arabia. In July 2002 Richard Perle caused an uproar when he introduced Laurent Murawiec, a RAND corporation analyst and former follower of Lyndon LaRouche, the notorious conspiracy theorist who moved effortlessly from the far left to the far right of American politics, to brief the Defense Policy Board. This elite advisory body listened in amazement as Murawiec explained that Saudi Arabia was 'the kernel of evil, the prime mover, the most dangerous opponent', and that, if necessary, 'what the House of Saud holds dear' – its oilfields and investments in the US, and even Islam's two holiest cities, Mecca and Medina – should be 'targeted'.[1]

In the ensuing furore Rumsfeld and Perle were quick to dissociate themselves from these ravings. But Murawiec's views are shared by others on the Republican right. According to Michael Ledeen of the American Enterprise Institute, 'the terror network – from al-Qaeda to Hizbollah, from Islamic Jihad to Hamas and various Palestine Liberation Organization groups – is as potent as it is because of the support given by four tyrannical regimes, which I term the "terror masters": Iran, Iraq, Syria and Saudi Arabia.' Ledeen doesn't actually propose that the US go to war against Saudi Arabia. He argues that Washington's first target should be Iran, which 'created, trained, protected, funded, and supported the world's most deadly terrorist group – Hizbollah'.[2] (The fact that Ledeen places Hizbollah, the radical Islamist movement that waged a successful guerrilla war to drive Israel from southern Lebanon, ahead of al-Qaeda says much about some neoconservatives' priorities: apparently killing Israeli soldiers is a more heinous crime than massacring American civilians.)

Some historical perspective is necessary in order to appreciate the astonishing reversal involved in placing Saudi Arabia in the same category as three of Washington's least favourite 'rogue states'. An intimate relationship with the Saudi monarchy has been one of the lynchpins of American global strategy since the end of the Second World War. As that conflict drew to a close, a meeting took place that symbolized both the shift under way from British to US hegemony in the Middle East and why the region matters so much to the Great Powers. In February 1945, on his way back from the Yalta summit with Winston Churchill and Joseph Stalin that effectively settled the postwar partition of Europe, the dying American president, Franklin Roosevelt, made a point of meeting the founder of the Saudi dynasty, King Ibn Saud, on a US Navy ship in the Suez Canal. The *New York Times* commented: 'The immense oil deposits in Saudi Arabia alone make that country more important to American diplomacy than almost any other nation.'[3]

Nearly sixty years after the meeting between FDR and Ibn Saud, a report by Human Rights Watch summarizes the continuing significance of what Gilbert Achcar has called 'an Islamic Texas' to the United States:

> For the United States, Saudi Arabia, as the world's largest oil exporter, is a vital ally. Over half the kingdom's crude oil exports, and the majority of its refined petroleum exports, go to Asia, while the US gets 17 per cent of its crude oil exports from Saudi Arabia. US civilian and military merchandise exports to the country in 2000 totalled $6.23 billion, according to the US embassy in Riyadh, and investments in the country by US-based multinationals are around $5 billion. Saudi investments in the US total nearly half a trillion dollars, mainly stocks and bonds, bank deposits, and real estate, according to US officials. Saudi Arabia is by far the top customer for US arms exports among developing countries, taking deliveries worth more than $28 billion in the 1993–2000 period, according to the latest annual report on arms transfers from the Congressional Research Service.[4]

The US–Saudi relationship is strategic as well as economic. In January 1980, in the wake of the Iranian Revolution and the Soviet intervention in Afghanistan, President Jimmy Carter announced what quickly came to be known as the Carter Doctrine (since Truman, any American president worth his salt has had to have his own doctrine): 'An attempt by any outside force to gain control of the Persian Gulf will be regarded as an assault on the vital interests of the United States of America, and such an assault will be repelled by any means necessary, including military force.'⁵ In line with this priority a new US Central Command was created with responsibility for Western Asia: it was to wage the two campaigns against Iraq as well as the war in Afghanistan. During the 1980s, the US and the Saudi regime worked closely together on two vital fronts. First, continuing a policy initiated by Carter's National Security Advisor, Zbigniew Brzezinski, the Reagan administration and their Saudi allies financed, trained and armed Islamist guerrillas to fight the Soviet occupation army in Afghanistan – a policy that produced the most spectacular case of blowback to date, since it was from the Afghan mujahedin that Osama bin Laden emerged. Secondly, Saudi Arabia openly and the US tacitly supported Iraq in its eight-year war with Iran in an effort to contain the Iranian Revolution.

During the 1980s the Saudis also spent heavily to build up their own military capabilities – though, as Lawrence Korb, Deputy Defense Secretary under Reagan pointed out, the chief beneficiary of this expenditure was the Pentagon: 'in effect, we had a replica of US airfields and ports over in that part of the world paid for by the Saudis to be used by the United States when and if we had to go over there.'⁶ These facilities proved very useful when Central Command deployed to Saudi Arabia after Saddam Hussein's invasion of Kuwait in August 1990. The 1991 Gulf War was fought by the US in very close alliance with the Saudi monarchy – understandably enough since the Iraqi seizure of Kuwait threatened to reduce the latter to, at best, a puppet of Baghdad. The dependence of Saudi security on American arms was reflected in the continued US military presence in Iraq after the 1991 war – yet another source of blowback, since, of course, the presence of infidel troops in the land of Islam's holiest places was one of the main grievances that prompted bin Laden to launch his terrorist campaign against the US.

Yet, despite the intimacy of the Saudi–American connection, Riyadh opposed the US conquest of Iraq. Moreover, for some American neoconservatives, victory in Iraq should prompt a move against, among other Arab regimes, the Saudi monarchy. Three factors are involved in this shift. First, there is 9/11. The Bush administration itself sought to skate over bin Laden's roots in the Saudi ruling class and the Saudi origins of fifteen of the nineteen 11 September hijackers, but many on the Republican right have been much more open in holding Saudi Arabia to account: 'The Saudis are active at every level of the terror chain, from planners to financiers, from cadre to foot soldier, from ideologist to cheerleader,' Murawiec told the Defense Policy Board.[7] Relatives of 9/11 victims launched a trillion dollar lawsuit against several Saudi institutions, and three members of the Saudi royal family for financing terrorism. In the distorted prism of the right-wing Republican worldview, 11 September has helped to shift Saudi Arabia into the axis of evil.

It is important to appreciate that the relationship between Washington and Riyadh has deteriorated on the Saudi side as well. In part this is for political reasons that predate 11 September. Even the corrupt and brutal Saudi royal family had to reflect the anger that grew throughout the Arab world during the 1990s because of US support for Israel and the Anglo-American blockade of Iraq. In February 1998, when the Clinton administration threatened to attack Iraq over disputes arising from the UN weapons inspection programme, Crown Prince Abdullah of Saudi Arabia pointedly told Secretary of State Madeleine Albright the following Bedouin tale:

A livestock owner, he related, whose flock was losing a lamb every three or four days to a wolf, was persuaded to buy 20 fierce guard dogs to keep the predator at bay. But then he found he had to slaughter three or four lambs every day to keep the guard dogs. Pausing for effect the Crown Prince is then supposed to have gone on: 'At that point the owner of the flock decided to get rid of the guard dogs and co-exist with the wolf, as this was the least costly and perhaps the least dangerous course.'[8]

The second Palestinian *intifada*, 9/11 and the drive for war on Iraq only made matters worse. In August 2002 the *Financial Times* reported that 'disgruntled Saudis' had withdrawn as much as $200 billion from the US in recent months, helping to push the dollar down. Among the reasons cited were anger at US support for Israel and the calls made by right-wing commentators for Saudi assets in the US to be frozen. 'Calls are now coming out of Riyadh, including in the press close to the government, urging a review of the strategic relationship with the US. A less public debate among Saudi Arabia's elite is whether to punish the US by pricing oil in euros rather than dollars.'[9]

Secondly, as we have already seen, to a much greater extent than was true of earlier generations of American conservatives, many contemporary right-wingers unconditionally support the state of Israel. This stance reinforced the neoconservatives' preoccupation with Iraq, long seen as a major threat by Israel. The Republican right's hostility to the Middle East peace process further leads them to detest conservative Arab states such as Saudi Arabia and Egypt for the pressure they put on Washington to force Israel back to the negotiating table. Murawiec proposed delivering an ultimatum to the Saudis demanding, *inter alia*, that they 'stop all anti-US, anti-Israeli predication [*sic*], writings, etc., within Arabia'.[10]

The right's alternative to negotiating with the Palestinians is forcibly to reshape the Arab world. At the height of the Jenin crisis in the spring of 2002 William Kristol and Robert Kagan argued that Bush should not allow himself to become 'so immersed in peace-processing' that he forgets 'the road that leads to real peace and security – the road that runs through Baghdad'.[11] Overthrowing Saddam would be the beginning of a process of 'rollback' – like the US-engineered counter-revolutions in Central America and the collapse of Stalinism in Eastern Europe during the 1980s – that would spread liberal democracy throughout the Arab world. According to the *Wall Street*

Journal, 'liberating Iraq from Saddam and sponsoring democracy would not only rid the region of a major military threat. It would also send a message to the Arab world that self-determination as part of the modern world is possible.' If this democratic upheaval replaced the House of Saud with an anti-American government, this 'would force a decision on whether to take over the Saudi oilfields, which would put an end to OPEC'.[12]

The conquest of Iraq certainly enormously enhances the capability of the US to pursue such adventures. Shortly before the Anglo-American invasion of Iraq, George Friedman of the private intelligence analysis company Stratfor wrote:

> On the day war ends, and if the United States is victorious, then the entire geopolitics of the region will be redefined. Every country bordering Iraq will find not the weakest formations of the Iraqi army along their frontiers, but US and British troops. The United States will be able to reach into any country in the region with covert forces based in Iraq, and Washington could threaten overt interventions as well. It will need no permission from regional hosts for the use of facilities, so long as either Turkey or Kuwait will permit transshipment into Iraq. In short, a US victory will change the entire balance of power in the region, from a situation in which the United States must negotiate its way to war, to a situation where the United States is free to act as it will . . . The conquest of Iraq will not be a minor event in history: It will represent the introduction of a new imperial power to the Middle East and a redefinition of regional geopolitics based on that power. The United States will move from being an outside power influencing events through coalitions, to a regional power that is able to operate effectively on its own. Most significant, countries like Saudi Arabia and Syria will be living in a new and quite unpleasant world.[13]

In the wake of victory, the neoconservatives were quick to argue that the US should immediately start flexing its muscles as a regional power. Michael Ledeen, for example, announced: 'The battle for Iraq is drawing to a close, but the war against terrorism has only just begun.' He claimed that 'both Iran and Syria are engaged in a desperate terrorist campaign against coalition forces in Iraq.' This reflected a 'strategy of a "second Lebanon"' allegedly outlined by the Syrian President Bashar al-Assad – that is, an approach modelled on the guerrilla campaigns mounted by the Shi'ite militias Amal and Hizbollah that drove first US and then Israeli forces out of Lebanon after the 1982 invasion. Ledeen proposed that Washington respond with 'regime change' through a political campaign that would start by targeting Syrian dominance of Lebanon but would encourage popular risings in Syria and Iran and thereby 'unleash democratic revolution on the terror masters in Damascus and Tehran'.[14]

Syrian hegemony over Lebanon dates back to the civil war of 1975–6. President Hafez al-Assad began to send Syrian troops into Lebanon in April 1976 in order to prevent the alliance of the left-wing Lebanese National Movement and the Palestine Liberation Organization defeating the Maronite Christian fascist militias. He did so on the basis of an understanding with both the US and Israel, who were also eager to prevent a victory by the Lebanese left and the Palestinian resistance: Syrian troops were acceptable so long as they did not cross a 'red line' in southern Lebanon. Syrian intervention tipped the balance in favour of the Maronite militias, who massacred 3,000 Palestinian civilians at the Tel al-Za'atar refugee camp in the summer of 1976, and in the longer term helped to create the relationship of forces that made possible the disastrous 1982 Israeli invasion of Lebanon.[15] The eventual consolidation, in the aftermath of that catastrophe, of Syrian hegemony over Lebanon in 1989–91 depended critically on a tacit deal between Assad and the elder Bush's administration that secured in exchange Syrian participation in the 1991 coalition against Saddam Hussein. The eagerness with which neoconservatives such as Ledeen now embrace the 'liberation' of Lebanon is, like their hostility to Saudi Arabia, an indication of their ambition to rewrite the existing map of the Middle East – a map that is covered in Washington's fingerprints.

It is here that the relationship between ideology and reality in the policies of the Bush administration are hardest to fathom. After the conquest of Iraq, how far do the Republican right want to go? The administration – like all its predecessors – is very far from being homogeneous. Policy decisions emerge through a process of sometimes intense internal struggle. The conflicts here in part involve the well-known battles – for example, over whether or not to seek United Nations authority for war on Iraq – that were waged by pragmatic multilateralists such as Colin Powell against more hawkish figures such as Dick Cheney, Donald Rumsfeld and Paul Wolfowitz.[16] But the latter group – even if united on the question of war with Iraq with or without the UN – has its own divisions. Ivo Daalder of the Brookings Institution is one of a number of analysts who distinguish 'assertive nationalists', traditional conservatives such as Cheney and Rumsfeld, from the 'democratic imperialists' – Wolfowitz and the rest of the neoconservative hard core. According to Charles Kupchan of the Council on Foreign Relations,

> Rumsfeld is fundamentally concerned with what goes on between these borders and will do what's necessary to keep America safe. Wolfowitz also cares about the safety of US territory, but sees it as part of a more ambitious programme of change.
>
> Wolfowitz is the intellectual leader of a version of [US] primacy that incorporates revolutionary aims in the sense of transforming the world in America's image. It's not just about American security and American pre-eminence; it's about using that pre-eminence to further a political programme.[17]

'In the Bush administration,' write Stephen Fidler and Gerald Baker, 'there has been an alliance of convenience on many issues between these two groups.' They could agree, for example, on higher defence spending and the shift away from multilateralism implied by the denunciation of the Kyoto protocol and the Anti-Ballistic Missile Treaty. Nevertheless, 'in the early days of the George W. Bush administration, it was Mr Cheney's brand of hard-nosed conservatism that trumped the neocons.' What pushed them together was 11 September. According to Kupchan, 'after 9/11, you don't see a lot of daylight between the democratic imperialists and the assertive nationalists. Pre-9/11, you did.'[18]

But now that the objective of regime change in Iraq has been achieved, divisions may open up again between these two groups. One problematic issue is 'nation-building' – the reconstruction of societies conquered by American military might. When campaigning for the presidency George W. Bush renounced such an aim on the basis of the Clinton administration's bad experiences in Somalia, Haiti and the Balkans. It is a policy that, for once, Rumsfeld and his generals are united in resisting. But inevitably the wars in Afghanistan and Iraq have dragged the US into building compliant regimes on the ruins of their overthrown predecessors. In the case of Afghanistan, the US has concentrated on maintaining Karzai in control of Kabul and fighting the remnants of al-Qaeda. Such a policy of malign neglect will be much harder to sustain in Iraq, a modern and relatively urbanized society with close links with the rest of the Arab world. Wolfowitz and his fellow neoconservatives positively welcome this opportunity that this necessary consequence of regime change offers to effect the transformation of Western Asia, as Kupchan puts it, 'in America's image'. Though this objective of 'democratic revolution' has been endorsed on occasion by both Bush and his National Security Advisor, pursuing it may well be productive of many conflicts in Washington.

A closely connected issue concerns the neoconservatives' demands that Washington follow the overthrow of

Saddam Hussein by replacing other Arab regimes. The least plausible candidate for regime change is surely the Saudi monarchy. The connections that bind it to the US are very deep, involving intimate economic ties between the two ruling classes. Ex-President George H. W. Bush and his former Secretary of State, James Baker, are both members of the Carlyle Group, a shadowy private investment company that has significant Saudi involvement. As fate would have it, the Carlyle Group had a meeting in Manhattan on 11 September 2001: thus it was that pillars of the American establishment stood side by side with one of Osama bin Laden's half-brothers, watching the Twin Towers crumble in flames and dust. It seems hard to believe that, despite the growing tensions between the two states, any administration would lightly overturn a regime with which US interests are so closely linked, particularly since the result might be to provoke an Islamist popular revolution. Similar considerations apply to Hosni Mubarak, President of Egypt, the most populous and important Arab country. Both the Saudi and Egyptian regimes are corrupt and brutal dictatorships with lamentable human rights records (indeed Mubarak is now mimicking the Saudi monarchy by grooming his son for the succession). But their very absence of popular support has the advantage that it has always had from Washington's point of view – the Cairo and Riyadh regimes have little choice but, with whatever complaints and qualms, to continue toeing the US line.

Much more in the firing line are Syria, ruled by the regional branch of the same Arab Ba'ath Socialist Party whose estranged Iraqi branch held power under Saddam Hussein, and the Islamic Republican regime in Iran. During the 2003 war Rumsfeld warned Syria and Iran against giving military aid to Iraq. After the collapse of Saddam's regime, Washington stepped up the pressure. Now it was Syria's chemical programme that was the problem, along with the refuge that Assad was allegedly giving to Iraqi leaders and weapons of mass destruction (how convenient that these should have somehow been shipped to Saddam's ancient enemies in Syria, thus explaining the paucity of evidence for them in Iraq itself). The Iranian regime was accused of covertly developing its own nuclear weapons programme, of offering sanctuary to al-Qaeda activists, and of meddling in Iraq. Coercive diplomacy, however, might serve Washington's purposes as well as another war, at least in the short term. After all, the strategic position of both states has been seriously weakened by the US military presence in Iraq.

There are, however, two good reasons for not ruling out the possibility of the US attacking Syria or even Iran. The first is the logic of the situation in occupied Iraq. The absence of any committed American allies with real roots in Iraqi society (with the exception of the Kurds in northern Iraq, whose political aspirations set them at odds with every state in the Middle East, with the possible exception of Israel) and the process of economic colonization for which the occupation regime provides a framework make it highly probable that the US and British forces will come into conflict with at least sections of the Iraqi population. The history of modern Iraq embraces huge popular mobilizations, powerful Communist, nationalist, and Shi'ite Islamist traditions, and vicious interethnic violence.[19] Now that the iron grip of Saddam's dictatorship has been removed, real Iraqi politics is beginning to assert itself in all its ambiguous vitality – increasingly against the occupation regime and its clients.

The precedent of Israel's occupation of southern Lebanon after the 1982 war may come to haunt Washington. The steady pinprick of military casualties – often by suicide bombings – forced the Israel Defence Force gradually to withdraw and finally to pull out altogether. Family links, as well as ideology, connect the Shia Muslim leaders in southern Iraq with Hizbollah, whose guerrillas drove Israel out of Lebanon. Should the US find itself in difficulty in Iraq, the temptation would be enormous to explain the failure of American policy by the malign influence of neighbouring 'terror states' and to adopt a policy that might begin with 'hot pursuit' and finish in attempts at conquest. The US invasion of Cambodia in 1970 and the long history of Israeli aggression against the Arab world provide plenty of precedents for such actions. In such an eventuality, the calls by ideologues such as Ledeen for 'democratic revolution' against the Syrian and Iranian 'terror masters' would provide a ready-made justification for yet more wars of 'liberation'. As Anatol Lieven puts it, 'the danger is not so much that the Bush Administration will consciously adopt the whole Neo-Con imperialist programme, as that the Neo-Cons and their allies will contribute to tendencies stemming inexorably from the US occupation of Iraq and that the result will be a vicious circle of terrorism and war.'[20]

There is a second reason for refusing to rule out the occurrence of more American wars, and that is the nature of the Bush administration itself. Precisely the same kind of case that was made against moving on to Syria after the fall of Baghdad – the military and political risks of war, the efficacy of the alternative strategy of containment – had informed the arguments for not attacking Iraq in the first place. At least one wing of the Bush administration is seriously committed to the imposition of what it deems to be democracy by American military might. Sometimes at least they have the ear of the President himself. In his court history of the Afghan War, Bob Woodward summarizes Bush's views thus: 'His vision clearly includes an ambitious reordering of the world through pre-emptive and, if necessary, unilateral action to reduce suffering and bring peace.'[21] This sounds pretty much like Wolfowitz's 'democratic imperialism' (perhaps with a dash of Tony Blair's 'humanitarian' version of the same ideology thrown in). After the conquest of Iraq, only a fool could confidently predict that George W. Bush has hung up his marching boots.

Blood and oil

The real underplot to the neoconservatives' triumphalist fantasies of imposing liberal democracy on the Middle East is provided by the third factor in the Republican right's thinking on the region – oil. It is the fact that Saudi Arabia contains the world's largest oil reserves (currently estimated at 261.7 billion barrels) that has bound together the American and Saudi ruling classes since the Second World War. Iraq has the world's second largest reserves, some 112.5 billion barrels. Some supporters of the 2003 war have sought to prove that it couldn't have been about oil through calculations intended to show that the market value of Iraq's reserves might be about the same as some estimates of the cost of conquering the country.[22] Such calculations, even if correct, do little more than provide further evidence – if it were needed – of how little of any importance profit-and-loss accounting tells us.

The economic significance of oil cannot be reduced to its market price – important as that is for those with claims on the profit and rent deductible from that price. Simon Bromley argues that Middle Eastern oil has been important to the US less because of its direct contribution to the American economy (which remained largely reliant on its own energy supplies till the late 1960s) than thanks to its function as a 'strategic commodity'. 'US control over world oil became a key resource in the overall management of its global leadership' after 1945, particularly given the greater dependence of the other main centres of Western capitalism – Europe and Japan – on imported oil.[23]

Daniel Yergin calls the era after the Second World War 'the Age of the Hydrocarbon Man': 'If it can be said, in the abstract, that the sun energized the planet, it was oil that now powered its human population, both in its familiar form as fuel and in the proliferation of new petrochemical products.'[24] As far as the administration of the younger Bush is concerned, let Hydrocarbon Man reign without end. An administration of oilmen (and the odd oil woman – Condoleezza Rice served on the board of directors of Chevron while the Republicans were out of office in Washington during the 1990s), it has been described by Mike Davis as 'the executive committee of the American Petroleum Institute'.[25] Bush's rapid denunciation of the Kyoto protocol indicated his commitment to an energy model based on the wasteful and environmentally destructive consumption of non-renewable fossil fuels. Indeed Anatol Lieven suggests that the war on Iraq was 'part of a larger strategy to use American military force to permit the continued offloading onto the rest of the world of the ecological costs of the existing US economy – without the need for any short-term sacrifices on the part of US capitalism, the US political elite or US voters'.[26] Just because of its commitment to the world that the fossil fuel corporations have made, the Bush administration was particularly concerned about US long-term access to energy supplies. In May 2001 Washington released the National Energy Plan drafted (with the help of Enron) by a team headed by Dick Cheney.

The Cheney report highlighted the growing dependence of the US on imported oil. Fifty-two per cent of America's net oil needs were met by imports in 1999. US oil consumption is expected to rise by 33 per cent by 2020, when declining domestic output would cover less than 30 per cent of the country's oil consumption. These trends would place the US in what the Cheney team called 'a condition of increased dependency on foreign powers that do not always have America's interests at heart'. Accordingly, 'energy security must be a priority of US trade and foreign policy.' The report recommended diversifying US sources of supply: Canada, Saudi Arabia, Venezuela and Mexico produced nearly 55 per cent of US oil imports in 2000. The Middle East, with perhaps two-thirds of global oil reserves, would 'remain central to world oil security', the report argued. 'The Gulf will be a primary focus of US international energy policy, but our engagement will be global, spotlighting existing and emerging regions that will have a major impact on the global energy balance' – notably the Caspian region, Russia and Africa. Washington should give US energy companies whatever backing they needed to gain access to these regions and to secure the development of the infrastructure they needed (for example, the pipelines to send Caspian oil and gas westwards).[27]

The Cheney team concerned itself with more than America's oil needs, as the reference quoted above to the 'global energy balance' indicates. The report stressed that 'a significant disruption in world oil supplies could adversely affect our economy and our ability to promote key foreign and economic policy objectives, regardless of the level of US dependence on oil imports'. It noted that 'oil demand is projected to grow three times as fast in non-OECD countries as in OECD countries, which will increase world-wide competition for global oil supplies.' Asia was likely to occupy a particularly important place in this competitive struggle, since it has less than 5 per cent of the world's proven oil reserves but is responsible for more than 10 per cent of oil production and about 30 per cent of oil consumption. More particularly, according to the Cheney team, 'China is a critical player in global energy security issues, since its net imports are expected to rise from approximately 1 million barrels per day at present to possibly 5 to 8 million barrels of oil per day by 2020, with a predominant (over 70 per cent) dependence on Middle East imports.'[28] Informing this analysis was a clear understanding of oil's role not simply in underpinning the American economic model but in maintaining US global hegemony.

Michael Klare writes that, since 11 September, 'whatever the original intent of American policy makers, the key strands of the administration's foreign security policy – the pursuit of imported petroleum, the enhancement of US "power projection" capabilities, and the war against terrorism – have now merged into a single strategic enterprise ... "the war for American supremacy".[29] The way in which these priorities dovetail in together is indicated by the fact that the three areas on which Washington has focused in the 'war on terrorism' – the Middle East, Central Asia and the Caucasus, and Latin America – are all regions with significant reserves of oil and/or natural gas. In Latin America, the Bush administration stepped up military aid to the Colombian government that had already begun under Clinton's Plan Colombia. US officials also initially supported the right-wing coup attempted against the radical nationalist regime of Hugo Chávez in Venezuela in April 2002. Both countries are, of course, important oil producers. More generally, Latin America's marked shift to the left, reflected most dramatically in Lula's victory in the Brazilian presidential elections in October 2002, has, according to the *Financial Times*, been received by the Republican right as 'tantamount to the extension of a new "axis of evil" that already includes Fidel Castro's Cuba and Hugo Chávez's Bolivarian revolution in Venezuela'.[30]

Zbigniew Brzezinski has called the area stretching from the Black Sea to the borders of China, India and Pakistan the 'Eurasian Balkans' – politically unstable and threatened by more powerful neighbours such as Russia, Turkey and Iran. The area is, like the European Balkans, 'a familiar combination of power vacuum and power suction' and thus 'geopolitically significant ... But the Eurasian Balkans are infinitely more important as a potential economic prize: an enormous concentration of natural gas and oil reserves are concentrated in the region, in addition to important minerals, including gold.'[31] Klare summarizes the penetration of this region by the US military since 9/11:

> the war on terrorism has also been merged with US efforts
> to safeguard the flow of Caspian oil and natural gas to

markets in the West. These efforts began on a modest scale during the Clinton administration, when the Department of Defense established links with the armed forces of Azerbaijan, Georgia, Kazakhstan, Kyrgyzstan, and Uzbekistan and began to provide them with military aid and training. But now, in the wake of September 11, these efforts have been significantly expanded. Hence, the temporary US bases in Uzbekistan and Kyrgyzstan are being transformed into semi-permanent installations, while US aid will be provided 'for the refurbishment of a strategically located air base' in Kazakhstan. According to the State Department, this move is intended to 'improve US–Kazakh military cooperation while establishing a US interoperable base along the oil-rich Caspian'. Azerbaijan will use American aid to establish a maritime defense capability in the Caspian Sea – the site of several recent encounters between Azerbaijani oil-exploration vessels and Iranian gunboats. While facilitating these countries' participation in the war against terrorism, these initiatives are also linked to US efforts to provide a safe environment for the production and transport of petroleum.[32]

US military intervention in the Middle East must be seen in the context of what Klare calls this 'strategy of global oil acquisition'. As we have seen, the relationship between the US and Saudi Arabia is deteriorating, on both sides. Saudi Arabia has played a critical role in the Organization of Petroleum-Exporting Countries, using its huge reserves to persuade other members of the cartel to keep production and prices at levels that maintain a steady inflow of revenue but don't bite too deep into the profits of the Western corporations or encourage investment in less efficient oil-bearing regions not controlled by OPEC. But even if the Saudi royal family continues to pursue this course, their oil isn't enough to fuel the US economy. The post-Saddam Iraqi government, placed and maintained in power by American arms, will be a feeble creature, highly responsive to Washington's pressures. Some oil experts believe that an American-dominated Iraq would pull out of OPEC. At the very least, it would pump up production, which has been depressed by the lack of investment in the oil industry since 1991 and the UN embargo, pushing down oil prices.[33]

Michael Renner points to a further benefit produced by the conquest of Iraq. During the oil crises of the 1970s, 'nationalization spread through the Middle East and OPEC nations. Today state oil companies own the vast majority of the world's oil reserves.' The great Western oil corporations – the 'super-majors' such as ExxonMobil and Royal Dutch-Shell – still dominate the industry down-stream in refining and distribution, but production from their oilfields accounted for only 35 per cent of their sales volume in 2001 and they own only 4 per cent of world reserves. Renner suggests: 'If a new regime in Baghdad rolls out the red carpet for the oil multinationals to return, it is possible that a broader wave of denationalization could sweep through the oil industry, reversing the historic changes of the early 1970s', to the great benefit of the 'super-majors'.[34] As we have seen, Rumsfeld and his pro-consul in Baghad have made privatization a priority.

One final advantage accruing from the control the Iraq War has given the US over the world's second largest oil reserves flows from its character as what Bromley calls a 'strategic commodity'. An American client regime in Iraq not only eases concerns about America's long-term access to oil; it also increases Washington's leverage over allies and rivals such as Germany and Japan that are even more dependent than the US on imported oil. In a larger context, the US military presence in the Gulf and Central Asia enhances Washington's ability if necessary to choke off oil and gas supplies to China, whose headlong growth has made its economy increasingly dependent on imported supplies of energy. Economic and geopolitical considera-tions are thus inextricably interwoven in the grand strat-egy of American imperialism.

− 5 −

Collision of Empires

Imperialism and Empire

Andrew Bacevich, a sceptical conservative academic − and ex-colonel in the US Armored Cavalry − wrote not long ago: 'although the United States has not created an empire in any formal sense − what would be the point of doing so? − it has most definitely acquired an imperial problem. This is the dirty little secret to which the elder George Bush, Bill Clinton, and George W. Bush each in turn refused to own up.'[1] In fact, the idea that the US is (or should become) an imperial power is far from a secret any more. It is affirmed with enthusiasm by right-wing commentators. Niall Ferguson, for example, writes: 'Political globalization is a fancy word for imperialism, imposing your values and institutions on others. However you dress it up, whatever rhetoric you may use, it is not very different in practice to what Britain did in the eighteenth and nineteenth centuries.'[2] Dana Priest reports that Donald Rumsfeld's office 'sponsored a private study of the great empires − Macedonia under Alexander the Great, Republican Rome, the Mongols − asking how they maintained their dominance? What could the United States learn from the successes and failures of ancient powers?'[3]

But for the concept of imperialism to be useful in understanding contemporary world politics its meaning must be clarified. 'Imperialism' has in fact broad and narrow meanings. In its broad sense it refers to the political, military and/or economic domination of small and/or weak countries by powerful states. This is a transhistorical conception of imperialism, as applicable to Sargon of Akkad as it is to George W. Bush. The narrower understanding of imperialism is more historically focused: formulated within the Marxist tradition, especially in the early twentieth century, it seeks to explain modern versions of imperialism in the broad sense on the basis of a historical understanding of the development of the capitalist mode of production. Its central claim was that, in unifying the planet, capitalism created a highly unequal world dominated by a handful of Great Powers that competed both economically and militarily. During the 1980s and 1990s, the Marxist theory of imperialism came to seem outdated: on the one hand, it suffered by apparent association with theories of Third World dependency, which were widely held to have been refuted by the rise of the East Asian 'Tiger' economies; on the other hand, the increasingly fashionable idea of humanitarian intervention implied that the Great Powers – at least when they were liberal democracies – could act out of benevolent motives and with beneficent results. But more recent experience suggests that this was too hasty a move. Imperialism is back with a vengeance: we need all the intellectual tools available to make sense of it.[4]

To get some idea of the kind of purchase the Marxist theory of imperialism can give, it may be worth situating it with respect to two other perspectives on international politics. The first is realism, probably the most intellectually consequent of the theoretical paradigms within mainstream academic studies of international relations. Realism views international politics as an anarchic order in which competing states conceived as rational actors pursue their security interests. Given influential formulations in the mid twentieth century by, among others, E. H. Carr and Hans Morgenthau, realism has more recently been cast in more analytically sophisticated forms by writers such as Kenneth Waltz and John Mearsheimer.[5] The second perspective takes various forms, but all have in common the idea that contemporary international politics has been transformed by globalization: economic interdependence, the emergence of forms of 'global governance', and the communications revolution made possible by information technology are progressively displacing the old system of interstate rivalries. This perspective is defended by many mainstream theorists, but it is also endorsed by more radical thinkers.

Thus Michael Hardt and Tony Negri draw a sharp contrast between traditional imperialism and the new form of political sovereignty that they call Empire, 'a *decentred* and *deterritorialized* apparatus of rule that progressively incorporates the entire global realm within its open, expanding powers'. Hardt and Negri deny that rivalries between the Great Powers are any longer a significant feature of a contemporary world transformed by global economic integration: 'what used to be conflict or competition among several imperialist powers has in important respects been replaced by the idea of a single power that overdetermines them all, structures them in a unitary way, and treats them under one common notion of right that is decidedly postcolonial and postimperialist.' Instead of imperialism with its rival centres of power, we have an impersonal, decentred network of power: 'In this smooth space of Empire, there is no *place* of power – it is everywhere and nowhere.'[6]

Like the more mainstream theories of political globalization with which it shares many common features, Hardt and Negri's conception of Empire expresses the belief, widely held in the 1990s, that, with the end of the Cold War, serious interstate conflict – at least among the major powers – was being transcended as national governments became more and more drawn into multilateral processes of 'global governance'. In any case, it is clear that the international crisis since 9/11 has decisively refuted this analysis. As we have seen, at the heart of this crisis have been the efforts of the Bush administration to use American military power to perpetuate the global dominance of the United States. In the process, they have split international institutions such as the UN and Nato, and provoked the emergence of what is beginning to look like a rival coalition to the Anglo-American duo, headed by France, Germany and Russia, with China tagging along on the side-lines – a development that I consider in more detail below.

The responses of Hardt and Negri to the refutation of their theory have been, to say the least, confused. Hardt has argued that 'the captains of capital in the US' should recognize that the Bush strategy isn't in their interests, and that 'there is an alternative to US imperialism: global power can be organised in a decentred form, which Tony Negri and I call "empire".'[7] So Empire isn't so much the political form of capitalist globalization as a policy option that enlightened capitalists should embrace. For Negri by contrast, Empire is not an alternative to the Bush war-drive but what explains it: 'Preventative war . . . is a constituent strategy of Empire.' At stake in the present crisis, according to Negri, are 'the forms of hegemony and the relative degrees of power that American and/or European capitalist elites will have in the organisation of the new world order'.[8] So, in contradiction to what Hardt and Negri argued in their book, Empire involves rival centres of capitalist power after all.

Relative to this muddle, realism seems – well, much more realistic in insisting on the continuity of what A. J. P. Taylor called 'the struggle for mastery' among the Great Powers.[9] Mearsheimer, for example, the leading theorist of 'offensive realism', is refreshingly free from the confusion, self-deception and hypocrisy that are so characteristic particularly of liberal supporters of the 'war on terrorism'. But realism too suffers from serious analytical inadequacies. Two in particular seem relevant here. First, realism tends to ignore the role that ideological representations play in motivating political action in both the domestic and the international arena. Thus Mearsheimer has been a forceful critic of the Bush administration's strategy since 11 September on the basis of an alternative reading of US interests and the best means of realizing them.[10] Irrespective of the validity of this criticism, it does not help us to understand the strategy that the Bush administration is pursuing, where ideological and strategic considerations are closely intermingled. More generally, even though it is the case that actors' interests aren't necessarily the same as their perceptions of those interests, one reason for the potential gap is that these perceptions are themselves ideologically constituted.[11]

Secondly, in treating states (conceived as unitary entities) as the sole significant international actors, realists fail to integrate into their analysis the capitalist economic context on which both Marxists and liberal enthusiasts for globalization lay such stress. Mearsheimer argues that hegemony can only be obtained at a regional and not a global level: the US, like Britain before it, is not globally hegemonic. Rather it is simply an 'offshore balancer' that, shielded by the Atlantic and Pacific, seeks to prevent regional hegemons emerging in Europe and Asia. This excessively restrictive conception of hegemony springs in part from the fact that Mearsheimer equates hegemony with the kind of absolute political domination that ancient empires such as Rome at least in principle exercised: 'A hegemon is a state that is so powerful that it dominates all the other states in the system.'[12] This definition makes it impossible to understand offshore balancing as one means of maintaining global hegemony. But more fundamentally, the capitalist economic context within which states operate gives them both resources to pursue their geopolitical objectives and further motives for taking action within the interstate system in order to advance the interests of the capitals based in their territory. Hegemony is better understood as the capacity, always relative and contested, of the most powerful state in the world system to get other states to support it in pursuing its objectives thanks to what Simon Bromley calls its 'structural power', 'which derives from advantageous positions within the various dimensions of the international system' – for example, the system of production, financial markets and 'the world military order'.[13]

One of the virtues of the Marxist theory of imperialism is that, because it is based on Marx's understanding of the capitalist mode of production, it conceptualizes the international in broader terms than realists do, without falling into the wishful thinking characteristic of liberal enthusiasts for globalization. It does so by treating the diplomatic and military conflicts among states as instances of the more general process of competition that drives capitalism on. More specifically, as formulated most rigorously by Nikolai Bukharin during the First World War, the theory of imperialism asserts that in the course of the nineteenth century two hitherto relatively autonomous processes – the geopolitical rivalries among states and economic competition between capitals – increasingly fused. On the one hand, the increasing industrialization of war meant that the Great Powers could no longer maintain their position without developing a capitalist economic base; on the other hand, the growing concentration and internationalization of capital caused economic rivalries among firms to spill over national borders and to become geopolitical contests in which the combatants called on the support of their respective states. Economic and security competition were now closely interwoven in complex forms of conflict that developed into the terrible era of interimperialist war between 1914 and 1945.[14]

It is this theory that provides the best framework for understanding the contemporary American war-drive. But before proceeding it is important to clarify one crucial point. Often both friends and critics of the Marxist theory of imperialism reduce it to the claim that states act exclusively from economic motives. One recent version of this is the widely held belief that the real aim behind the Western attack on Afghanistan was the desire of the Bush administration and the oil corporations to which it is closely allied to build a pipeline through Afghanistan as a means of exporting the oil and gas of Central Asia.[15] Now, undoubtedly the energy reserves of the region are an important factor in Washington's interest in the region, but to reduce the war in Afghanistan to this interest would be a bad mistake. The US attacked Afghanistan primarily for political reasons focused on reasserting its global hegemony after 11 September; the greater access it gained to Central Asia was an important by-product of the overthrow of the Taliban, not the main motive behind this action.[16] Similarly, the Bush Doctrine can't simply be read off the administration's corporate connections: rather, it represents a more or less coherent project for maintaining and strengthening US hegemony that has, *inter alia*, an economic dimension – control over Middle Eastern oil is, as we have seen, a major preoccupation in the Bush administration's war planning.

More generally, throughout the history of modern imperialism, Great Powers have acted for complex mixtures of economic and geopolitical reasons. At the end of the nineteenth century the British ruling class began to perceive Germany as a major threat to their interests, in the first instance because of the decision by the Second Reich to build a world-class navy. This was a threat to Britain's naval supremacy, and to the security of the British Isles themselves, but control of the empire – and of the flows of profits from overseas investments – was closely bound up with British sea power.[17] To take another example, Hitler was an intensely ideological ruler, whose long-term aim was to secure dominance of the Eurasian landmass for a racially purified Germany, but economic considerations played a powerful role both in military strategy (the decisions to start the Second World War, to extend it to the Soviet Union, and to attempt to take Stalingrad were heavily influenced by fears about raw material shortages) and in Hitler's vision of a colonized Russia as the solution to the economic contradictions of German capitalism.[18] American global strategy since the Second World War has also involved both economic and geopolitical calculations, as I showed in chapters 3 and 4. The Marxist theory of imperialism analyses the forms in which geopolitical and economic competition have become interwoven in modern capitalism, but does not seek to collapse these analytically distinct dimensions into one another.[19]

The peculiarities of American imperialism

In the light of this theoretical perspective, let us now consider what is distinctive to the United States as an imperial power; in doing so I refer frequently to the writings of Giovanni Arrighi, which, in setting American hegemony in world-historical perspective, provide a valuable and stimulating foil. Analysts often argue that American imperialism functions, on a much larger, global scale, as its British predecessor did. Economically the US practises a version of the imperialism of free trade on which Victorian Britain relied, using its politico-military power to ensure that world markets are sufficiently open to allow its capital and commodities to flow relatively freely: the role that institutions such as the International Monetary Fund and World Bank play in implementing the neoliberal Washington Consensus has to be seen in the light of what Bacevich calls this 'strategy of openness'.[20] Geopolitically, as we have seen, the US operates as an offshore balancer, sheltered by the seas and intervening to prevent a rival hegemon or hegemonic coalition emerging in Eurasia. Like Britain in its heyday, it has relied on a dual strategy, manipulating the balance of power in Europe and Asia and relying on naval and air forces sustained by a global network of bases to project power where necessary.[21]

Both Britain and the US have maintained relatively small land armies, which they commit to major wars on the Eurasian landmass only with great reluctance. Even during the supreme contest of the Second World War Franklin Roosevelt kept the US Army to 90 divisions rather than the 215 that military planners believed were required to defeat Germany and Japan, thereby tacitly relying on the Soviet Union to provide the manpower (and take the casualties) needed to defeat Hitler. A preoccupation with minimizing American casualties in US policy-making thus predates the Vietnam Syndrome.[22] The British naval bombardment of Copenhagen with cannon and Congreve rockets in August 1807, which killed nearly 2,000 civilians and outraged international opinion (Thomas Jefferson took it as evidence that 'the 1800s were, with the Macedonian and Roman imperial eras, one of "three epochs in history characterized by the total extinction of national morality"') proved to be the prototype of an Anglo-American pattern of conquest by long-distance destruction – from Hamburg, Dresden and Hiroshima, through the devastation of Korea and Vietnam during the Cold War, to the more recent bombing campaigns against Iraq, Yugoslavia and Afghanistan.[23] The enlightened spirit informing this reliance on airpower was expressed by Lloyd George's comment on the British government's argument at the 1932 Disarmament Conference that bombing was 'necessary for police purposes in outlying places' (i.e. colonial possessions such as India and Iraq): 'we insisted on reserving the right to bomb niggers!'[24]

Historical analogies are useful only so long as we are aware of their limits. Against the background of the theoretical framework outlined in the previous section and the parallels just noted, let us now consider what is specific to US imperialism. First, the ability of the United States to operate globally depended on its establishing hegemony over, and expelling rivals from the Americas. As John Mearsheimer puts it,

American foreign policy throughout the nineteenth century had one overarching goal: achieving hegemony in the Western Hemisphere. That task, which was motivated in good part by realist logic, involved building a powerful United States that could dominate the other states of North and South America and also prevent the European great powers from projecting their military might across the Atlantic Ocean.[25]

This grand strategy, pursued by the American political elite throughout the nineteenth century, involved the acquisition of vast swathes of territory through the Louisiana Purchase of 1803 and the defeat of Mexico in the war of 1846–8, the spread of settlers across the continent, and the conquest and virtual extirpation of the Native American peoples. Senator Henry Cabot Lodge boasted that the US had 'a record of conquest, colonization, and territorial expansion unequalled by any people in the nineteenth century'.[26] This process put the US in a position actually to enforce the Monroe Doctrine, enunciated in 1823 and seeking the exclusion of European powers from the Americas. The turning point probably came in 1895–6, when President Grover Cleveland aggressively took up Venezuela's side in a border dispute with British Guiana. Rather contradicting the doctrine that liberal democracies never fight one another, the British prime minister, Lord Salisbury, wrote in January 1896: 'A war with America – not this year but in the not too distant future – has become something like a possibility.'[27] It was Britain that eventually backed down. As Mearsheimer puts it, 'the United Kingdom and the United States ended their long rivalry in North America in the early twentieth century. In effect, the United Kingdom retreated across the Atlantic Ocean and left the United States to run the Western Hemisphere.'[28]

The obverse of the exclusion of outside powers was the political and strategic subordination of the other states of the Americas to the US. Henry Kissinger comments on President Woodrow Wilson's invocation in January 1917 of the Monroe Doctrine as a model for his projected League of Nations: 'Mexico was probably astonished to learn the president of the country which had seized a third of its territory in the nineteenth century and had sent its troops into Mexico the preceding year was now presenting the Monroe Doctrine as a guarantee of the territorial integrity of sister nations and as a classic example of international cooperation.'[29] Nor is this merely a historical irony to savour. The strategic priority of preserving US hegemony in the Americas is sufficient without any anti-Communist ideological commitments to explain Washington's efforts to isolate Cuba since the 1958 revolution, successfully to remove (where it had failed with Fidel Castro) the Sandinista regime that held power in Nicaragua between 1979 and 1990, to defeat other radical nationalist movements in Central America, to invade Panama in 1989 and seize its ruler, Manuel Noriega, and to send troops to Haiti in 1994. After the conquest of Iraq, the contemporary left-wing upsurge in Latin America may well come to preoccupy Washington strategists.

There is, secondly, an important difference between how British capitalism in its heyday was inserted into the world economy and the position occupied by the United States. As Giovanni Arrighi, Kenneth Barr and Shuji Hisaeda put it, 'in the last quarter of the nineteenth century, the British system of business enterprise was more than ever an ensemble of highly specialized medium-sized firms held together by a complex web of commercial transactions – a web that was centred on Britain but spanned the entire world.' There was an elective affinity between 'this extroverted, decentralized, and differentiated business structure' and the geographically dispersed character of the British Empire, with its formal and informal colonies spread across five continents. Not simply was the economic structure of American capitalism – the 'system of vertically

integrated, bureaucratically managed multinational corporations' – very different from that of its British predecessor, but it was far more insulated from the world
economy.[30] America's vast continental economy, and the
resources and skills to which it has access within its own
borders, continue to mean that the share of exports in US
national income – about 10 per cent – is still relatively
small compared with, say, the European Union average of
20 per cent. The huge home market gives American multinationals a strong domestic base from which to trade and
invest abroad. These characteristics also, according to
Arrighi, Po-keung Hui, Krishnendu Rai and Thomas
Ehrlich Reifer, gave the US a selective advantage in the
great interimperialist struggles of the first half of the twentieth century:

> The global dispersion and weak mutual integration of
> Britain's colonial domains – as opposed to the regional
> concentration and strong mutual integration, both polit-
> ical and economic, of the territorial domains of the
> twentieth-century United States – is the most important
> difference in the spatial configuration of the two hege-
> monic states . . . Britain's far-flung territorial empire was
> an essential ingredient in the formation and consolidation
> of the nineteenth-century British world order. But as soon
> as interstate competition for 'living space' intensified
> under the impact of the transport revolution and the
> industrialization of war, the protection costs of Britain's
> metropolitan and overseas domains, and Britain's world-
> encompassing empire turned from an asset into a liability.
> At the same time, the overcoming of spatial barriers
> brought about by these same two phenomena turned the
> continental size, compactness, insularity, and direct access
> to the world's two major oceans of the United States into
> decisive strategic advantages in the escalating interstate
> power struggle.[31]

The other two peculiarities of American imperialism are
of more recent vintage. Thirdly, then, Britain at the height

of its empire ran a large balance of payments surplus that allowed it to export capital on a vast scale. This surplus concealed the fact that Britain actually ran a deficit on trade: it was income from investments and from services such as banking, insurance and shipping, and Britain's surplus with India that produced an overall payments surplus with the rest of the world.[32] However arrived at, the surplus allowed Britain to finance the very extensive overseas investments, both direct and portfolio, that knitted its global economic interests together. Between 1870 and 1914 British foreign investment averaged from 4 to 5 per cent of national income a year, rising to 9.3 per cent in 1910–13.[33] One sign of Britain's decline was the role that the US assumed after both world wars of funding (in the case of the Marshall Plan by direct aid rather than loans) European economic recovery. But here there is a decisive difference between the political economy of the Pax Britannica and that of American imperialism today, at the beginning of the century that it would like to make its own. The United States has over the past generation come to suffer from chronic balance of payments deficits that have made it a net importer of capital. Arrighi provides figures illustrating this transformation of the US

from being the main source of world liquidity and foreign direct investment, as it has been in the 1950s and 1960s, into the world's main debtor nation and absorber of liquidity, from the 1980s to the present . . . In the five-year period 1965–69 the account still had a surplus of $12 billion, which constituted almost half (46%) of the total surplus of the G7 countries. In 1970–74, the surplus contracted to $4.1 billion and to 21% of the total surplus of the G7 countries. In 1975–79, the surplus turned into a deficit of $7.4 billion. After that the deficit escalated to previously unimaginable levels: $146.5 billion in 1980–84; $660.6 billion in 1985–89; falling back to $324.4 billion in 1990–94 before swelling to $912.4 billion in 1995–99 . . .[34]

The external payments deficit is simply one of a series of financial imbalances that structure the contemporary American economy. During the boom of the 1990s, the private sector – both households and firms – were heavily into debt. Firms shedding unprofitable investments and workers since the present recession began in 2000 are pushing business back into surplus (at the price of rising unemployment) but households remain heavily indebted. The federal government is also running a rapidly increasing budget deficit that the Bush administration's policies of tax cuts and higher military spending are bound to increase.[35] There might seem to be a natural association between financial indebtedness and geopolitical decline. After all, Britain's need to sell off overseas assets and borrow heavily from the United States to fight the two world wars is generally seen both as an index of its inability to confront the economic and military challenge constituted by Germany and as key stages in the transition from one hegemon to another. But here there is another remarkable difference, the fourth that sets apart American imperialism from its predecessor. Far from declining relative to the other Great Powers over the past generation, the US has ascended since the end of the Cold War to the status of 'hyperpower' (as the former French foreign minister Hubert Vedrine put it). This is most evident in the military dimension, where both the level of the Pentagon's spending and the extent and quality of its military capabilities put it in a different category from every other state in the world. Such military supremacy was never true of Britain even at the height of its nineteenth-century hegemony, when London concentrated on maintaining global naval superiority but balanced between continental European powers with greatly superior land armies.

The result is an extraordinarily contradictory situation. Martin Wolf argues that the rest of the world's willingness to hold US assets at a relatively high exchange rate with the dollar would be critical to cushioning the financial impact of the war in Iraq on American taxpayers:

This depends, to a large extent, on Asia. It is the Asians, not the US, who have a 'strong dollar' policy, for it is they, together with other foreign investors, who have both the ability and the desire to avoid a fall in the dollar against their currencies. Indirectly, the rest of the world still pays for the exercise of US power.

In 2002 . . . the US ran a current account deficit of $498 billion. Meanwhile, the Asia-Pacific region ran a surplus of $204 billion, contributed largely by Japan, with a surplus of $113 billion, Taiwan and mainland China, both with $21 billion, Singapore with $17 billion, and Hong Kong with $17 billion . . . Western Europe ran a surplus of $115 billion, of which the eurozone's share was $45 billion . . . The picture on current accounts is reinforced by that on official currency reserves. At the end of the third quarter of last year [2002], total foreign currency reserves were $2,294 billion, 73 per cent of which were held in dollars. Some 58 per cent of these reserves were held by Asian governments. Japan alone held 19.3 per cent of the total and mainland China another 11.3 per cent.[36]

'The sinews of war are Asian,' in John Plender's words.[37] The capacity of the Bush administration to pursue its global 'war against terrorism' while seeking actually to cut taxes depends on the complaisance of Asian governments willing to carry on accumulating stupendous amounts of US government paper. For Arrighi this represents a serious anomaly. As he and his collaborators note,

the present transition [from one hegemonic power to another] has been characterized not by a *fusion* of a higher order, but by a *fission* of military and financial power. Control over globally effective means of violence has become ever more concentrated than it was in the hands of the declining hegemon. But control over universally accepted means of payment is increasingly concentrated in the hands of transnational business agencies or (mostly East Asian) governmental agencies of no political or military significance and far removed from the traditional

(Euro-American) power centres of the modern world system.[38]

This anomaly, Arrighi and Beverley Silver conclude, implies ambiguous prospects:

> *The most important geopolitical novelty of the present hegemonic crisis is a bifurcation of military and financial capabilities that has no precedent in earlier hegemonic transitions. The bifurcation decreases the likelihood of an outbreak of war among the system's most powerful units. But it does not reduce the chances of a deterioration of the present hegemonic crisis into a more or less long period of systemic chaos.*[39]

The sense of paradox that Arrighi expresses here is in part a consequence of the quasi-cyclical philosophy of history that informs his often highly illuminating research and leads him to interpret every systemic crisis as a transition from one hegemonic power to another that instantiates long-term patterns expressed in both repetitions and variations.[40] Once we liberate ourselves from this theoretical straitjacket it becomes easier to make sense of the 'bifurcation of military and financial capabilities' that the Asian-funded American war-drive undeniably dramatizes. It is best seen as the consequence of a trend that one might call the partial dissociation of military and economic competition, which developed within the Western bloc after the Second World War. A division of labour emerged during the Cold War, in which the US (and Britain) ran much higher levels of arms spending than did Germany and Japan. This arrangement had several functions. It allowed the US to maintain overall geopolitical leadership over power centres – Western Europe and Japan – that might otherwise develop into serious rivals. In exchange, the defeated Axis powers were allowed to recover in a form that was less likely to upset their neighbours than full-blooded rearmament, and that provided a degree of economic stability and coherence to strategically crucial regions. Finally, the very high levels of arms expenditure by peacetime standards maintained by the US while the Cold War was at its most serious in the 1950s and 1960s helped to make possible the long economic boom of those decades both by preventing the development of a crisis of profitability and by maintaining effective demand at historically elevated levels.[41]

Their much lower military expenditure allowed the economies of Western Europe (with the exception of Britain) and Japan to invest heavily in advanced means of production in civilian industries. High rates of investment in these sectors and their then relatively low-paid workforces allowed them increasingly to undercut their American rivals and thereby to shift the balance of trade in their favour. As the Cold War de-escalated in the course of the 1960s, Europe and Japan began to be seen by American policy-makers as free riders who, cushioned by the Pentagon's military power, were stealing US markets. The Vietnam War exacerbated the US balance of payments crisis and thereby helped to push the dollar down on the foreign exchanges. Under the Nixon presidency (1969–74) the US hit back, ending the dollar's convertibility against gold, pulling American ground troops out of Vietnam, pursuing détente with the USSR and a strategic partnership with China, and sharply cutting back on military spending. The effect was, among other things, to divert resources back into investment in civilian industries. Global growth soared in the early 1970s in a climate of intensified competition and accelerating inflation leading to a squeeze on profitability the offsetting mechanisms to which had been weakened by the reductions in arms spending.

These developments ushered in what Robert Brenner calls the 'long downturn' – the era of slow economic growth that has lasted to the present day. The US has pursued two kinds of strategy during this period. On the one hand, it has sought to enhance its economic position relative to its rivals-and-allies in the European Union and

East Asia. Domestically, this has involved a brutal process of restructuring that has imposed continuous reorganizations on American corporations and exercised powerful downward pressures on wages and working conditions. Internationally, US economic strategy has tended to focus on efforts to manipulate the dollar – sometimes downwards, in order to enhance the competitiveness of American exports and the profitability of US manufacturing, as in the late 1970s and between 1985 and 1995, sometimes upwards, notably in the strong dollar policy pursued more or less consistently by the Clinton administration from the mid-1990s onwards (but now apparently abandoned by its successor), which made it easier to attract the foreign capital needed to fund the chronic balance of payments deficit.

On the other hand, the US – as we have already seen in chapter 3 above – has sought to maintain its political and military leadership over the Western capitalist bloc. This has periodically involved sharp increases in American defence spending as part of a larger assertion of Washington's global power. This was true, for example, during the so-called Second Cold War, which began under Carter in the late 1970s and continued under Reagan until Gorbachev's efforts to reform the Soviet Union began to undermine the superpower partition of the world. The administration of the younger Bush marks another phase of higher defence spending and more general US self-assertion. As a result of these trends, the US lead in military expenditure has been institutionalized into a permanent pattern – though relative to American, let alone global national income, even the gigantic defence budgets demanded by Bush and Rumsfeld are too small to play the kind of stabilizing role that their predecessors did in the 1950s and 1960s. The US defence budget is now greater than those of the next twenty-five military powers combined, but US defence spending has dropped as a share of national income from around 15 per cent during the Korean War to successively lower peaks in each later burst of military expenditure: 12 per cent in the late 1950s, 10 per cent during the Vietnam War, 7–8 per cent in the mid-1980s, and only 4 per cent in early 2002.[42]

Relative to this long-term pattern, one might argue that the phases of military assertiveness by Washington represent quite a rational exploitation of one of the United States's main comparative advantages. Now that euphoria surrounding the American boom of the late 1990s has evaporated, and the elements of speculation and straight-forward fraud are being exposed, the claims made for the US 'New Economy' – that its performance had taken it 'beyond history', as Alan Greenspan, chairman of the Federal Reserve Board put it – have deflated along with the Wall Street bubble. Brenner points out that US productivity growth during the boom 'was not decisively better than that of its leading rivals. Whereas between 1993 and 2000 manufacturing labour productivity improved at an annual average rate of 5.1 per cent, manufacturing labour productivity in western Germany and France grew at the annual average rates of 4.8 per cent (through 1998) and 4.9 per cent respectively.'[43] Richard Layard extends the comparison to economies as a whole: 'In the past ten years output per hour worked has grown faster in euro-zone countries than in the US, and in France and Germany it is now as high as it is in the US. Even on a per capita basis, output has grown as fast in the euro-zone as in the US – over the past ten years and over the past three.'[44] According to the International Monetary Fund, in 2001 not only Germany and France but also Italy had higher output per hour than the US.[45] That same year, the European Union's merchandise trade with the rest of the world was 18.3 per cent of the global total, while that of the US was 19.5 per cent.[46] America's huge military lead over the other powers should not be allowed to conceal the fact that the economic contest, particularly with the European Union, is much more evenly balanced.

What are the consequences of this discrepancy between the military and economic position of the US? Arrighi argues that 'the main reason why the monetarist counter-revolution [under Carter and Reagan] was so successful in reversing the decline of US power is that it brought about a massive rerouting of global capital flows towards the United States and the dollar' that contributed to a broader 'financialization' of American capitalism.[47] Though Arrighi does not put it in these terms, this assessment invites a view of the US almost as an imperial parasite that is able to attract foreign capital and maintain its hegemony through a kind of protection racket underpinned by its military power.[48] But such an interpretation omits two crucial considerations. First, the US recovery in the later 1980s and the 1990s involved a real reorganization of the productive economy expressed particularly in the greater international competitiveness of the IT sector: the 'New Economy' hype that surrounded the 1990s boom should not be allowed to obscure the improvement in the condition of productive capital that it represented.[49]

Secondly, the Asian capitalisms that hold vast quantities of American dollars – even though US interest rates are relatively low – do not do so out of fear of the Pentagon's might but for reasons of their own self-interest. This apparently economically irrational strategy is in fact largely a case of what has been called 'exchange-rate protectionism'. Thus Japanese banks and corporations by investing in dollar assets – with strong government encouragement – help to keep the yen's exchange rate relatively low and thereby to maintain Japanese competitiveness. American and Asian capitalisms are bound together economically by a complex web of mutual interdependence.[50] The same is true on a global level. To a significant extent the neoliberal policies pursued by the international financial institutions have, by opening hitherto relatively closed economies to foreign trade and investment, provided public goods for European and Japanese as well as American multinationals. It was, for example, French companies such as Suez and Vivendi that took advantage of the worldwide campaign to privatize water.

A return to interimperialist rivalries?

It is against this background – of a United States that is militarily but not economically pre-eminent – that we must consider the dramatic confrontation that developed between the US (loyally seconded by Britain) and the other Great Powers over the Iraq War. There is an astonishing contrast here between the scope of the coalition mounted against Iraq by the elder Bush in 1991 – which was sanctioned by the United Nations Security Council and involved the military participation of Egypt, Saudi Arabia and Syria – and the 'coalition of the willing' that his son led to war twelve years later. In 2003 only three countries – the US, Britain and Australia – took part in the fighting; Arab states (with the exception of Kuwait, a statelet whose very survival as an independent entity had rested on American bayonets) and Washington's Nato partner Turkey shunned the war; and, among the leading powers, France, Germany and Russia led the opposition on the Security Council, with China offering them cautious support in the background. Though the outcome of the 2003 war provided further confirmation of US military capabilities, the threadbare character of the 'coalition' that allegedly prosecuted it represented a severe political and diplomatic defeat for Washington (albeit one mitigated by the fact that the administration do not seem to have fought hard for Security Council support, leaving Tony Blair and his ministers to hustle unsuccessfully for votes).

It was the way in which the Bush strategy seemed to be isolating the US internationally that attracted strong criticism from within the American establishment. In autumn 2002 James Baker and Lawrence Eagleburger, both Secretaries of State under the elder Bush, and Brent Scowcroft, National Security Advisor to both Ford and Bush *père*, publicly opposed unilateral military action against Iraq on the grounds that it would divert attention from and undermine support for the campaign against Islamist terrorism, and also destabilize the Middle East.[51] The critics were joined by senior figures in the Clinton administration such as Madeleine Albright and Richard Holbrooke, as well as by veterans of earlier presidencies such as Henry Kissinger and Zbigniew Brzezinski. This debate between the Bush administration and its critics tended to be more about tactics than objectives. Holbrooke, for example, endorsed the goal of 'regime change' in Iraq, but argued: 'The road to Baghdad runs through the United Nations Security Council.'[52]

Essentially this amounted to a return to the strategy of the first Bush administration in the lead-up to the 1991 Gulf War – using UN authority to legitimize the American exercise of military power, or, as Robert Kagan put it, 'the unilateralist iron fist inside the multilateralist velvet glove'.[53] Scowcroft and Brzezinski argued along very similar lines.[54] The administration moved some way in this direction with Bush's speech to the United Nations General Assembly on 12 September 2002. But the President and his advisers made it clear that they saw a new Security Council resolution as a prelude to military action against Saddam rather than, as France and Russia hoped, an alternative. Bush taunted the UN with the fate of the League of Nations, which was unable to prevent the outbreak of the Second World War, and warned: 'We will work with the UN Security Council for the necessary resolutions. But the purposes of the United States should not be doubted. The Security Council resolutions will be enforced . . . or action will be unavoidable. And a regime that has lost its legitimacy will also lose its power.'[55] The UN could either rubber stamp Washington's war or sit by and watch the US and Britain attack Iraq anyway.

In the event, of course, the US and Britain were unable to win a majority in the Security Council. The emergence of an antiwar alliance between France, Germany and Russia represented Brzezinski's worst nightmare. His entire geostrategy for maintaining US dominance of Eurasia involved promoting EU and Nato expansion in order to isolate Russia and encourage a Germany closely aligned to the US to assert a dominant role in Europe, with France playing a valued but subordinate role. Brzezinski had described a 'grand European realignment, involving either a German-Russian collusion or a Franco-Russian entente', let alone 'a European-Russian accommodation to exclude America from the continent', as 'improbable'. 'They would require not only a massive mishandling by America of its European policy but also a dramatic reorientation on the part of the key European states.'[56] But, over Iraq, all three potential challengers – France, Germany and Russia – united against war under French leadership. No wonder that Brzezinski complained that 'our single-minded and rather demagogic fixation on Iraq is undermining the credibility as well as the legitimacy of US leadership.'[57]

How significant, then, are the divisions that opened up among the Great Powers over the Iraq War? In his critique of US foreign policy under Clinton, Samuel Huntington discussed the possibility of 'the formation of an anti-hegemonic coalition involving several major powers'.[58] Is this what we are now seeing beginning to emerge? Or – to put it in terms of the classical Marxist theory of imperialism discussed earlier, are interimperialist rivalries developing in which the economic conflicts that undoubtedly exist between the US and the EU, for example, start to assume a geopolitical form? The answer is that the fracture exposed by the Iraq War is serious and probably long-lasting, but that it is unlikely to lead, in the short term at any rate, to the emergence of a serious geopolitical challenger to American hegemony.

In the first place, the antiwar bloc was an alliance of convenience rather than a long-term coalition. Jacques Chirac, Gerhard Schröder and Vladimir Putin are all arch-opportunists with not a principle between them. In the German case, electoral considerations – dictated by the unpopularity of the Red–Green coalition that barely squeaked back into office in the federal elections of

September 2002 and was under enormous pressure from business interests to mount an offensive against the welfare state – predominated in a rudderless and introverted government. Both Russia and France had economic interests in Iraq that the American conquest might threaten, and both had longer-term geopolitical reasons for seeking to counterbalance American hegemony. But the Putin regime's policy since 9/11 had generally been one of giving support to the US – for example, facilitating the entry of its forces into Central Asia, partly in order to win concessions on other issues, and partly to gain international legitimacy for its own brutal counterinsurgency campaign in Chechnya by reframing it as part of the global 'war against terrorism'.[59] The collapse of the Soviet Union has left Russia too economically weak and geographically isolated (thanks to the loss of Ukraine and the Transcaucasus, the most important acquisitions of the Romanov dynasty) to do anything more than manoeuvre between the US and the other Great Powers in order to maximize its influence. It was the role of France – still a significant military power and a permanent member of the UN Security Council – that was critical in cementing the antiwar bloc.

Secondly, to understand Chirac's willingness to push the confrontation over Iraq to the point of threatening to veto a resolution authorizing war one has to set French policy in the larger context of the development of the European Union. Since the Treaty of Rome in 1957, European integration has represented, not the transcendence of national antagonisms, but the framework within which the leading continental states have pursued their interests.[60] The process has been driven by a Franco-German alliance. The leaders of the Federal Republic have seen participation in European institutions as a means of pursuing German interests in a form less likely to arouse fears from its neighbours than more straightforward national self-assertion. For France, by contrast, the European project has represented both a potential counterweight to American hegemony and a means of mobilizing the resources that France requires to continue to operate as a world power. The Maastricht Treaty of 1991, which led to a very significant step forward in the integration process in the shape of European monetary union, involved a particularly delicate compromise between French and German interests: the Deutsche Mark was sacrificed in exchange for strict controls on public spending and borrowing and the establishment of an autonomous European Central Bank as the guardian of monetary orthodoxy – a deal that, as it turned out, has been a major contributor to Germany's economic stagnation since the euro was finally launched at the beginning of 1999.

The controversy over the Iraq War dramatized the fact that this Franco-German dominated EU is now under serious threat. This is in large part because of the very success of Brzezinski's strategy of expanding the EU and Nato as a means of maintaining and extending US hegemony. In 2004 ten new member states are due to join the EU, mostly Eastern and Central Europe countries ruled by political elites that, in the process of reinventing themselves as supporters of liberal capitalism, generally identify strongly with US global interests. In the lead-up to the Iraq War Donald Rumsfeld famously dismissed French and German opposition as 'old Europe. If you look at the entire Nato Europe today, the centre of gravity is shifting east.'[61] That this was no idle threat was underlined in February 2003, when ten East and Central European governments signed a statement drafted by Bruce Jackson, an ex-US military intelligence officer, that supported war on Iraq.[62]

Chirac reacted with fury, denouncing the East Europeans' bad manners and even hinting he might veto Romania's and Bulgaria's accession. Though he did not act on this threat, the vehemence of the French response indicated that Rumsfeld's 'New Europe' was a potential political reality. Britain's participation in the Iraq War, though defended with particular stridency by Tony Blair, was intelligible in terms of the strategy consistently pursued by British governments since Pearl Harbor of seeking to retain a global role for Britain through close alliance with the US.[63] The result had been to place Britain, even after its entry into the European Economic Community in 1973, in a Janus-faced position, looking across both the Atlantic and the Channel, that left her relatively isolated in European councils. But now – with right-wing governments in Italy and Spain, and most of the accession states also backing Washington – a British-led pro-American axis might outvote France and Germany. Indeed, argues George Friedman,

> the harder France and Germany pressed to create a common European front against the United States over Iraq, the more uneasy the rest of Europe became. Rather than decreasing support for the United States, Franco-German pressure forced many European countries that would have rather remained silent into the American camp. Ultimately, the current alignment reflects the fact that most Europeans would rather get their national security from a distant, powerful United States that is unlikely to try to subordinate their national identities than from a weaker but closer set of powers with whom they must have economic relationships but which frighten them as well.[64]

The conflict over Iraq therefore developed into a struggle among European elites over the future of the EU – *pace* Friedman, European public opinion was solidly antiwar, and the protests were largest in the three leading 'New Europe' countries, Britain, Italy and Spain. Through the fracture it has made visible in the EU, the Bush administration's global strategy has made continuing conflict between the US and, at the very least, France probable over the medium term. Philip Stephens, an editorialist normally close to 10 Downing Street, writes:

> Among the most important geopolitical shifts of the past two years has been the US administration's judgement that its interest now lies in dividing rather than uniting Europe.

Among the most depressing has been the way in which European governments have colluded in the fracturing of the continent. Washington's segregation of erstwhile allies into friends and enemies is intended as a blunt assertion of American primacy. In the long term the strategy will prove to be corrosive of US power. In the short term it has worked. Europe is in disarray.[65]

Thirdly, then, the outcome of these conflicts will probably not be a unified European imperialism that rivals American power. Such a development would require both greater cooperation between Europe's two leading military powers, Britain and France, and very substantial and sustained increases in defence expenditure by the EU states. Neither condition is likely to be met in the short term. The 1998 St Malo agreement between Britain and France created a framework for greater cooperation to enhance European military capabilities, but has remained largely a dead letter because of disagreements about whether or not such cooperation should allow the EU to operate independently of Nato – something that Paris, but not London (let alone Washington), favours. More generally, it is highly improbable that Britain and the other 'New Europe' governments would favour a defence programme that would be intended as an alternative to following US leadership. The very cause of transatlantic conflict – the development of pro- and anti-American axes *within* the EU – makes it much harder for Europe to develop as an independent military power. But even if the European political elites were agreed on the desirability of such a development, the domestic obstacles would be formidable. The ill-named European Growth and Stability Pact, agreed in 1996 within the framework of the Maastricht Treaty, imposes very tight controls on public spending and borrowing within the euro-zone that are already causing enormous strains on social provision in continental Europe. As long as these controls are in place, any attempt significantly to increase military spending would have to cut deeply into the welfare state, provoking immense resistance. A shift to the Reagan–Bush *fils* style of military Keynesianism would free the EU from this dilemma and allow it to have guns and at least some butter, but such a policy shift would require a more direct threat to European security than is presently foreseeable.

As a result, international politics is likely to take the form it has largely maintained since the end of the Cold War, what Huntington calls 'a strange hybrid, a uni-multipolar system with one superpower and several major powers'.[66] The US is by far the strongest state in the world, particularly militarily, but it is by no means omnipotent. Even when it goes to war, it cannot act alone. In the 'war of terrorism' the Pentagon has depended on the cooperation of other states – Britain to provide both greater legitimacy and some useful combat units (the British armed forces are becoming America's Gurkhas – professional soldiers who are almost as reliable as, but more expendable than Americans), and others (for example, Pakistan, Uzbekistan, and Qatar) as logistical bases for military operations. Economically, as we have seen, the US operates on a much more level playing field. In institutions such as the International Monetary Fund and the World Trade Organization, Washington may be the first among equals, but it can only secure its goals through a process of often intensely contested bargaining particularly with the EU and Japan. The major capitalist states are bound together in relations and institutions that involve a complex and constantly shifting balance between cooperation and competition.[67]

Against this background it should be clear that it is oversimplistic to dismiss the present American administration's plans as irrational. As I have tried to show, the Bush team's strategy is based on a largely accurate reading of the long-term economic and geopolitical threats facing US capitalism, and involves the decision to exploit 11 September and America's current military supremacy to shift the global distribution of economic and political power further to its advantage. Behind this is impatience with the costs of the multilateral cooperation that was much more strongly emphasized under the elder Bush and Clinton – and perhaps also a sense of frustration produced by awareness that some cooperation is, as we have seen, simply unavoidable. An oscillation between multilateralism and unilateralism is a structural feature of American foreign policy. If the Bush strategy contains irrational elements – above all arising from the growing links between the American and Israeli right – it does not follow that the entire approach is just a Dr Strangelove-style adventure. Contested though the strategy may be within the ruling class, it represents one take on how best to advance the global interests of American capitalism.[68]

Yet the policy so far has made the world *less* manageable by Washington. The drive to pre-emptive military action against Iraq produced the most serious split among the Great Powers since the end of the Cold War, partly because it strengthened already existing fears in Paris, Berlin and Moscow about too unilateral a US hegemony, partly because the emergence of a pro-American axis within the EU threatens Franco-German dominance of European politics. France, Germany and Russia are not strong enough, or strongly motivated enough to develop a rival coalition, but they are likely to continue to manoeuvre against the Anglo-American bloc. And, of course, waiting on the sidelines is China: observing developments since 9/11 its rulers must now have a more powerful incentive to develop their military capabilities further at the same time as the country's headlong economic growth gives them the resources to do so. Moreover, conflicts between the US and the EU over trade are multiplying at the WTO. This is a recipe for what Arrighi and Silver call 'a more or less long period of systemic chaos'.

Catastrophe immanent

Meanwhile, far from the fields of outright combat in Afghanistan or Iraq, the world of neoliberal capitalism rolls on its usual course. The dominant fact about this world is not the 'war against terrorism', but the remorseless growth of poverty and inequality. The statistical evidence assembled by the philosopher Thomas Pogge is stomach-turning. Out of the 5,820 million human beings alive in 1998, 1,214 billion had an income of less than one US dollar a day, and 2.8 billion were living on less than $2 a day, the poverty line set by the World Bank. Eighteen million people die prematurely each year from poverty-related causes, one-third of all human deaths. Pogge calculates that 250 million people have died of starvation and preventable diseases in the fourteen years since the end of Cold War: 'The names of these people, if listed in the style of the Vietnam War Memorial, would cover a wall 350 miles long.'[69]

Mass poverty persists in the context of growing global inequality: the ratio of the income of the richest fifth of the world's population to that of the poorest fifth has risen from 30:1 in 1960 to 60:1 in 1990 and 74:1 in 1997.[70] This represents the manifest failure of the Washington Consensus, according to which liberalizing markets might lead to wider economic inequality but, because of the dynamic growth generated, would also raise the incomes of the poor. But a premiss of this argument has been refuted: the neoliberal era has seen a fall in growth rates. Not long ago William Easterly of the World Bank acknowledged the 'significant puzzle' that, despite neoliberal 'policy reforms' that 'should have led to accelerating, not falling growth', median per capita growth in the developing countries fell from 2.5 per cent per annum in 1960–79 to zero per cent in 1980–99.[71]

The fact that the obscenity of mass poverty is allowed to persist is an index of the priorities of the rich and the powerful. Pogge calculates that inequality – particularly between North and South – is now so great that a mere 1 per cent of aggregate global income, equivalent to $312 billion a year, would be sufficient to eradicate severe poverty worldwide.[72] This sum is less than the US defence budget: the Bush administration requested $380 billion for the Pentagon in the fiscal year 2004. Of course, the 'war on terrorism' is not the only war that destroys lives and wealth. Largely forgotten by the rest of the world, the struggle over the Democratic Republic of the Congo – rich in resources, but in little else – had cost, according to the International Rescue Committee, between 3.1 and 4.7 million lives by early 2003.[73] The wars of the poor do not attract live television coverage or embedded reporters; these are reserved for the wars of the rich.

It is hard not to believe that this is a world heading for catastrophe. The 'war on terrorism' can contribute materially to this process. The assertion of naked American military power will feed the hatred and despair that helped to produce the 11 September atrocities in the first place. The geopolitical instability and Great Power rivalries that the conquest of Iraq has promoted will encourage states large and small to look for the weapons and tactics that will give them an edge against the Pentagon. Which state, moreover, will be the next to adopt the Bush doctrine of unilateral preventive war against some neighbouring competitor? And what are the odds that someone somewhere – perhaps the US under its new more flexible nuclear plans – will actually resort to using weapons of mass destruction? Finally what would victory in this doubtful struggle against terrorism mean? Such a victory would allow American free-market capitalism to continue on its course, with even greater confidence than it displayed during the economic boom in the 1990s – while all the time poverty and inequality grew to even more disastrous levels, and the processes of environmental destruction that are fed by the US economy's ravenous appetite for fossil fuels accelerated.

No – to borrow the phrase that George Bush Senior used to denounce Saddam Hussein's invasion of Kuwait – this will not stand. Nemesis awaits the 'democratic imperialists' in the Pentagon, as it did earlier conquerors. The only question concerns the form that retribution will take. Will the imperial war machine finally fall by bringing on the great catastrophe that market capitalism has long been secreting within itself, in the process destroying the rest of us, and perhaps the earth itself as well? Or will collective political action bring the great juggernaut to a halt, as it did the Pentagon's attempt to subjugate Vietnam? The gigantic international movement that sprang up against the Anglo-American war on Iraq suggests that this latter hope is not entirely idle. Indeed, it is all the stronger because of the origins of this antiwar movement in the resistance to capitalist globalization that became visible in the Seattle protests of November 1999. For the fusion of these two causes, opposition to war and to neoliberalism, conjures up the possibility that, in the face of catastrophe, we may finally put an end to the capitalist system itself, with its logic of relentless competition for profit and power, before it drives us all over the precipice.

Epigraph

These and countless other events of this kind were brought to pass from time to time . . . by the operation of Adrastia, who punishes evil and rewards good deeds and whom we also call Nemesis. She is the sublime manifestation of a powerful divinity dwelling, men believe, above the orbit of the moon. Others define her as the personification of a protective power, exercising a general surveillance over the destinies of individuals, and represented in the theogonies of old as the daughter of Justice, who from her unseen eternal throne looks down upon all things on earth. Queen over all causation and arbiter and umpire of all events, she controls the urn from which men's lots are cast and regulates their vicissitudes of fortune, often bringing their enterprises a different end from that which they designed and confounding their various actions by the changes she imposes. It is she, too, who binds the vainly swelling pride of mortal men in the indissoluble chain of necessity, and casts, as she alone can, her weight on the scale by which they rise and fall; at one moment she bears down upon the stiff necks of the proud and takes away their strength, at another she raises the good out of the dust and exalts them to prosperity.

Ammianus Marcellinus, *The Later Roman Empire*

Notes

Prologue: At War between the Two Rivers

1 E. Gibbon, *The History of the Decline and Fall of the Roman Empire* (3 vols, Harmondsworth, 1995), vol. 1, pp. 931–2.
2 M. Mann, *The Sources of Social Power*, vol. 1 (Cambridge, 1986), p. 133.
3 Ammianus Marcellinus, *The Later Roman Empire*, ed. and trans. W. Hamilton (Harmondsworth, 1986), Book XXIV, sections 5, 7.
4 Ibid., XXV.1.
5 Gibbon, *History*, vol. 1, p. 945.
6 *House of Commons Debates*, 7 Apr. 2003, col. 25.
7 Ammianus, *Later Roman Empire*, XXV.4.
8 J. Keegan, *The Mask of Command* (Harmondsworth, 1988), Conclusion (quotation from p. 339).
9 'President Discusses the Future of Iraq', 26 Feb. 2003, www.whitehouse.gov.
10 'Ex-CIA Director: US Faces "World War IV"', 3 April 2003, www.cnn.com.
11 *Financial Times*, 14 May 2003.
12 L. F. Kaplan and W. Kristol, *The War over Iraq* (San Francisco, 2003), pp. 124–5.

13 G. Agamben, 'Une guerre contre l'Europe', *Le Figaro*, 8 Apr. 2003.

14 P. Tyler, 'A New Power in the Streets', *New York Times*, 17 Feb. 2003.

1 The Rhetoric of Conquest

1 Quoted in B. Woodward, *Bush at War* (New York, 2002), p. 44.

2 George W. Bush, 'Address to a Joint Session of Congress and the American People', 20 Sept. 2001, www.whitehouse.gov.

3 C. Johnson, *Blowback: The Costs and Consequences of American Empire* (New York, 2000), pp. 8, 33.

4 Quoted in T. Ali, *The Clash of Fundamentalisms* (London, 2002), pp. 208–9. This book, together with Gilbert Achcar's *The Clash of Barbarisms* (New York, 2002), is very helpful in providing a basis on which to appraise and respond to 9/11.

5 It is greatly to be regretted that as distinguished a philosopher of the left as Norman Geras should have fallen in with the 'moral equivalence' topos: see his interview in *Imprints*, 6:3 (2003).

6 Quoted in N. Chomsky, 'Who Are the Global Terrorists?', in K. Booth and T. Dunne, eds, *Worlds in Collision* (Houndmills, 2002). See also Chomsky, *9-11* (New York, 2001).

7 See Robert Fisk's account in his classic *Pity the Nation* (Oxford, 1991), chs 7–12.

8 Liberty, *Anti-Terrorism Legislation in the United Kingdom*, www.liberty-human-rights.org.uk, p. 4.

9 Ibid., p. 5.

10 Terrorism Act 2000, s. 59.

11 *Guardian*, 1 Apr. 2003.

12 'The President's State of the Union Address', 29 Jan. 2002, www.whitehouse.gov.

13 J. Bolton, 'Beyond the Axis of Evil', 6 May 2002, www.state.gov.

14 See, for example, M. E. Brown et al., eds, *Debating the Democratic Peace* (Cambridge, Mass., 1996).

15 J. Derrida, *Voyous* (Paris, 2003), ch. 6 (quotation from p. 101).

16 Ibid., p. 138 ('rogue' and 'rogue state' in English in the original).
17 S. Huntington, 'The Lonely Superpower', *Foreign Affairs*, Mar.–Apr. 1999 (online edition), www.foreignpolicy2000. org. Compare N. Chomsky, *Rogue States* (London, 2000).
18 L. F. Kaplan and W. Kristol, *The War over Iraq* (San Francisco, 2003), p. viii.
19 See, for example, the letter by Professor Ulf Bernitz and fifteen other academic international lawyers, *Guardian*, 7 Mar. 2003.
20 H. Morgenthau, *Politics among Nations* (New York, 1954), p. 281: see also ibid., p. 284, and Derrida, *Voyous*, p. 142.
21 J. J. Mearsheimer and S. J. Walt, 'An Unnecessary War', in M. L. Sifry and C. Cerf, eds, *The Iraq War Reader* (New York, 2003), pp. 419–20. For an example of the kind of prowar case criticized here, see Kaplan and Kristol, *The War over Iraq*, chs 1–3.
22 J. Battle, ed., 'Shaking Hands with Saddam Hussein: The US Tilts toward Iraq, 1980–1984', *National Security Archive Briefing Book*, no. 82, 25 Feb. 2003, www.gwu.edu/Ensarchiv. In their critical survey of the 'narrow realism' that the US displayed towards Saddam under Reagan and the elder Bush till August 1990 Kaplan and Kristol somehow manage to omit Rumsfeld's role: *The War over Iraq*, pp. 39–42.
23 Quoted in M. Curtis, *Web of Deceit* (London, 2003), p. 34.
24 'Statement by the Prime Minister, Tony Blair, House of Commons', 24 Sept. 2002, www.fco.gov.uk.
25 S. M. Hersh, 'Who Lied to Whom?', *New Yorker*, 31 Mar. 2003 (online edition), www.newyorker.com.
26 'Iraq Weapons Dossier "Rewritten"', 29 May 2003, www.news.bbc.co.uk.
27 J. S. Nye, *The Paradox of American Power* (Oxford, 2002), table 1.2, p. 36.
28 See Bruce Cumings's admirable account in *Korea's Place in the Sun* (New York, 1997), pp. 465–87.
29 See, for example, D. Kang, 'North Korea Has a Point', *Financial Times*, 3 Jan. 2003.
30 L. Freedman, 'A Strong Incentive to Acquire Nuclear Weapons', *Financial Times*, 9 Apr. 2003.

31 T. G. Carpenter, 'Nuclear Reaction to North Korea', *Financial Times*, 13 Dec. 2002.

32 Amnesty International, 'Central Asia: No Excuse for Escalating Human Rights Violations', 11 Oct. 2001, www.web.amnesty.org.

33 D. Priest, *The Mission* (New York, 2003), p. 39.

34 Human Rights Watch, *World Report 2003*, www.hrw.org.

35 T. Ali, 'The Colour Khaki', *New Left Review*, series II, 19 (2003).

36 'President Discusses the Future of Iraq', 26 Feb. 2003, www.whitehouse.gov.

37 Kaplan and Kristol, *The War over Iraq*, pp. 108–9.

38 J. Dower, *Embracing Defeat* (London, 2000), pp. 561, 560, 273. See also J. Halliday, *A Political History of Japanese Capitalism* (New York, 1975).

39 *Financial Times*, 29 Apr. 2003.

40 R. Dreyfuss, 'Tinker, Banker, NeoCon, Spy', *American Prospect*, 18 Nov. 2002, and D. Leigh and B. Whitaker, 'Financial Scandal Claims Hang over Leader in Waiting', *Guardian*, 14 Apr. 2003. Much information about the INC's hopelessly unsuccessful attempts, with increasingly sceptical CIA support, to overthrow Saddam will be found in A. Cockburn and P. Cockburn, *Saddam Hussein: An American Obsession*, rev. edn (London, 2002).

41 *The National Security Strategy of the United States of America*, Sept. 2002, www.whitehouse.gov, p. iv.

42 Ibid., pp. 17, 18.

43 Ibid., pp. 27, 1.

44 See, for example, D. Held, *Models of Democracy*, 2nd edn (Cambridge, 1996).

45 P. Bobbitt, *The Shield of Achilles* (London, 2002), pp. 228, 230.

46 Ibid., pp. 238–9.

47 *Guardian*, 12 Mar. 2003, 15 Apr. 2003, 8 May 2003.

48 'Remarks as Delivered by Secretary of Defense Donald H. Rumsfeld', Council of Foreign Relations, New York, 27 May 2003, www.defenselink.mil.

49 P. Mattera, 'Postwar Iraq: A Showcase for Privatization?', *Focus on Trade*, no. 86 (Apr. 2003), www.focusweb.org, pp. 9–10.

50 *Financial Times*, 23 and 24 May 2003.
51 Ibid., 27 May 2003.
52 A. Roy, 'Instant-Mix Imperial Democracy', 13 May 2003, www.cesr.org.
53 For example, C. Hitchens, 'Why I Am for Regime Change', in Sifry and Cerf, *The Iraq War Reader*.
54 M. Walzer, 'Five Questions about Terrorism', *Dissent* (Winter 2002) (online edition), www.dissentmagazine.org.
55 M. Walzer, 'Can There Be a Decent Left?', *Dissent* (Spring 2002).
56 M. Walzer, 'So, Is This a Just War?', *Dissent* (Spring 2003) (online edition), www.dissentmagazine.org.
57 T. Blair, 'Doctrine of International Community', speech to the Economic Club of Chicago, 22 Apr. 1999, www.fco.gov.uk.
58 'Remarks by the President and Other Participants in Democratic Leadership Forum The Third Way: Progressive Government for the Twenty First Century', 25 Apr. 1999, www.whitehouse.gov, p. 17. For further discussion, see A. Callinicos, *Against the Third Way* (Cambridge, 2001), esp. chs 2 and 3.
59 T. Blair, 'Speech to the Labour Party Conference', 2 Oct. 2001, www.labour.org.uk. For reasons of presentation, I have run together the sentence-long paragraphs in the original.
60 Ibid.
61 For arguments supporting this claim, see A. Callinicos, *Equality* (Cambridge, 2000) and *An Anti-Capitalist Manifesto* (Cambridge, 2003).
62 On the Republican right's social outlook, see W. Greider, 'Rolling Back the Twentieth Century', *The Nation*, 12 May 2003 (online edition), www.thenation.com.
63 T. W. Pogge, *World Poverty and Human Rights* (Cambridge, 2002), ch. 8 (quotation from p. 204).
64 David Runciman offers a detailed critique of Blair's conception of politics in 'The Politics of Good Intentions', *London Review of Books*, 8 May 2003.
65 M. Ignatieff, 'The Burden', *New York Times Magazine*, 5 Jan. 2003.
66 R. Cooper, 'The Post-Modern State', in M. Leonard, ed., *Re-ordering the World* (London, 2002), pp. 15, 16.
67 Ibid., p. 17.

68 D. Bensaïd, *Le Nouvel Internationalisme* (Paris, 2003), p. 131.

2 The Cultists of Eternal War

1 R. Wolff, 'The Bush Doctrine', *Financial Times*, 21 June 2002.

2 'Remarks by the President at 2002 Graduation Exercise of the United States Military Academy, West Point, New York', 1 June 2002, www.whitehouse.gov.

3 *National Security Strategy*, p. 6.

4 'X' (G. Kennan), 'The Sources of Soviet Conduct' (1947), in Kennan, *American Diplomacy* (Chicago, 1951), pp. 119, 120. See, among a now vast literature, D. Yergin, *Shattered Peace* (Harmondsworth, 1980) and J. L. Gaddis, *Strategies of Containment* (Oxford, 1982).

5 For a well-informed journalistic account, see Cockburn and Cockburn, *Saddam Hussein*.

6 C. Rice, 'Campaign 2000 – Promoting the National Interest', *Foreign Affairs*, Jan.–Feb. 2000 (online edition), www.foreignpolicy2000.org.

7 Interview in *Financial Times*, 23 Sept. 2002.

8 See the forceful argument for the continuation of a policy of containing Iraq in Mearsheimer and Walt, 'An Unnecessary War'.

9 Useful overviews of the administration's global policy will be found in N. Lemann, 'The Next World Order', *New Yorker*, 1 Apr. 2002, F. Fitzgerald, 'George Bush and the World', *New York Review of Books*, 26 Sept. 2002, A. Lieven, 'The Push to War', *London Review of Books*, 3 Oct. 2002, S. Fidler and G. Baker, 'America's Democratic Imperialists', *Financial Times*, 6 Mar. 2003, E. Drew, 'The NeoCons in Power', *New York Review of Books*, 12 June 2003, and J. Feffer, ed., *Power Trip* (New York, 2003). The Carnegie Endowment for International Peace has assembled a valuable collection of documents on the origins of the 2003 war at http://www.ceip.org/files/Iraq/index.htm#regime_change.

10 See Fred Halliday's account of the US counter-revolutionary offensive during the 1980s in *Cold War, Third World* (London, 1989).

11 H. Kissinger, *Diplomacy* (New York, 1994), p. 774.

12 A. Shlaim, *The Iron Wall* (London, 2001), p. 487.

13 'Excerpts from Pentagon's Plan: "Prevent the Re-Emergence of a New Rival" ', *New York Times*, 8 Mar. 1992; also at www.pbs.org: 'Excerpts from 1992 Draft *Defense Planning Guidance*'.

14 H. Kissinger, *Years of Renewal* (London, 1999), p. 175; see ibid., ch. 27 on Rumsfeld's bureaucratic sabotage of SALT II.

15 B. Woodward, *Bush at War*, pp. 21–2.

16 Fitzgerald, 'George Bush and the World', p. 84.

17 M. Lind, 'The Weird Men behind George W. Bush's War', *New Statesman*, 7 Apr. 2003 (online edition), www.newstatesman.com.

18 See especially A. Wald, *The New York Intellectuals* (Chapel Hill, 1987), and the debate between Wald and Lind on neoconservatism and Trotskyism at www.hnn.us.

19 L. Strauss, *The Rebirth of Classical Political Rationalism*, ed. T. L. Pangle (Chicago, 1989), p. 146. Shadia Drury explores Strauss's connections with neoconservatism in *Leo Strauss and the American Right* (Houndmills, 1997).

20 S. M. Hersh, 'Selective Intelligence', *New Yorker*, 12 May 2003.

21 Quoted in D. Yergin, *The Prize* (London, 1993), p. 607.

22 Institute for Advanced Strategic and Political Studies, 'A Clean Break: A New Strategy for Securing the Realm', 8 July 1996, www.israeleconomy.org.

23 Project for the New American Century, 'Statement of Principles', 3 June 1997, www.newamericancentury.org.

24 Project for the New American Century, Letter to President Clinton on Iraq, 26 Jan. 1998, www.newamericancentury.org.

25 Quoted in R. Ramesh, ed., *The War We Couldn't Stop* (London, 2003), p. 18.

26 Quoted in Woodward, *Bush at War*, pp. 49, 60; see ibid., ch. 6, for an account of the Camp David meeting. Rumsfeld reacted angrily when reminded of his 12 September remarks in an interview with the *Washington Post*: ibid., p. 319.

27 N. Lemann, 'How It Came to War', *New Yorker*, 31 Mar. 2003 (online edition), www.newyorker.com.

28 G. Kessler, 'US Decision on Iraq has Puzzling Past', *Washington Post*, 12 Jan. 2003.

29 Quoted in Lemann, 'How It Came to War'.

30 G. Friedman, 'Smoke and Mirrors: The United States, Iraq and Deception', Jan. 2003, www.stratfor.com.

31 *Financial Times*, 3 May 2003.

32 'Remarks as Delivered by Secretary of Defense Donald H. Rumsfeld', Council of Foreign Relations, New York, 27 May 2003, www.defenselink.mil.

33 'President Bush Announces Combat Operations in Iraq have Ended', 1 May 2003, www.whitehouse.gov.

3 The Grand Strategy of the American Empire

1 A. Lieven, 'The Push to War', p. 8.

2 J. Fallows, 'The Unilateralist: A Conversation with Paul Wolfowitz', *Atlantic Monthly*, Mar. 2002 (online edition), www.theatlantic.com.

3 E. Luttwak, *Strategy*, 2nd edn (Cambridge, Mass., 2001), p. 89. Luttwak first developed his version of the concept in *The Grand Strategy of the Roman Empire* (Baltimore, 1976).

4 The analysis outlined in this and the following paragraph draws on a number of essays published in a collection edited by G. John Ikenberry, *American Foreign Policy: Theoretical Essays*, 4th edn (New York, 2002) – notably two by Ikenberry himself, 'Rethinking the Origins of American Hegemony' (1989) and 'America's Liberal Grand Strategy' (2000), and M. P. Leffler, 'The American Conception of National Security and the Beginnings of the Cold War' (1984). Many of the findings in these essays were anticipated in Gabriel Kolko's pioneering work of radical historical scholarship *The Politics of War* (New York, 1970). Walter Russell Mead has written an important study of the ideologies of American foreign policy: *Special Providence* (New York, 2001).

5 T. Smith, 'National Security Liberalism and American Foreign Policy' (2000), in Ikenberry, *American Foreign Policy*, p. 258.

6 A. J. Bacevich, *American Empire* (Cambridge, Mass., 2002), pp. 2, 3.

7 Kaplan and Kristol, *The War over Iraq*, ch. 6 (quotation from p. 65).

8 Kissinger, *Diplomacy*, p. 813.

9 Ibid., p. 805.

10 See especially A. Callinicos et al., *Marxism and the New Imperialism* (London, 1994), and G. Achcar, 'The Strategic Triad' (1998), reprinted in T. Ali, ed., *Masters of the Universe?* (London, 2000).

11 See C. Harman, *Explaining the Crisis* (London, 1984), ch. 3, and R. Brenner, 'The Economics of Global Turbulence', *New Left Review*, series I, 229 (1998).

12 See, for example, K. E. Calder, *Asia's Deadly Triangle* (London, 1997).

13 J. J. Mearsheimer, *The Tragedy of Great Power Politics* (New York, 2001), p. 398.

14 Ibid., p. 400.

15 Brzezinski, *The Grand Chessboard* (New York, 1997), ch. 6 (quotation from p. 159). For a similarly sceptical assessment of the Chinese threat, see Nye, *The Paradox of American Power*, pp. 18–22.

16 C. Harman, 'Beyond the Boom', *International Socialism*, series 2, 90 (2001), and R. Brenner, *The Boom and the Bubble* (London, 2002).

17 Bacevich, *American Empire*, p. 105. See ibid., pp. 181–95 for an acerbic assessment of the 1999 Balkan War.

18 J. Rees, 'Nato and the New Imperialism', *Socialist Review*, June 1999; G. Achcar, 'Rasputin Plays at Chess' and P. Gowan, 'The Euro-Atlantic Origins of Nato's Attack on Yugoslavia', both in Ali, *Masters of the Universe?*

19 A. Callinicos, 'The Ideology of Humanitarian Intervention', in Ali, *Masters of the Universe?*

20 Brzezinksi, *The Grand Chessboard*, p. 10.

21 Ibid., pp. 31, 40, 198 (emphasis in the original). Brzezinski's 'geostrategy' for Eurasian domination is heavily influenced by Halford Mackinder, the academic geographer and Unionist MP who developed at the beginning of the twentieth century a conception of Eurasia as the 'World-Island' central to the struggle between the Great Powers: see H. J. Mackinder, *Democratic Ideals and Reality* (London, 1919). Joseph Nye, an ex-Clinton administration official, by contrast argues for a generally and genuinely multilateralist approach by the US: see *The Paradox of American Power*.

22 R. Kagan, 'Multilateralism, American Style', *Washington Post*, 13 Sept. 2002.

23 Quoted in Johnson, *Blowback*, p. 217.
24 Bacevich, *American Empire*, pp. 47, 49.
25 'Remarks by National Security Advisor Condoleezza Rice on Terrorism and Foreign Policy', 29 Apr. 2002, www.whitehouse.gov.
26 Quoted in N. Lemann, 'The Next World Order', *New Yorker*, 1 Apr. 2002 (online edition), www.newyorker.com.
27 Woodward, *Bush at War*, p. 282.
28 D. Acheson, *Present at the Creation*, (New York, 1969), p. 375; Truman quotation on p. 222.
29 See J. Chace, *Acheson* (Cambridge, Mass., 1998), ch. 16 (quotation from p. 168).
30 Thus Kaplan and Kristol praise NSC-68, the famous 1950 document setting out the Truman administration's strategy at the height of the Cold War: *The War over Iraq*, p. 65. For an internal critique of NSC-68, see Gaddis, *Strategies of Containment*, ch. 4.
31 P. Wolfowitz, 'Bridging Centuries: Fin de Siècle All Over Again', *National Interest*, 47 (1997) (online edition), www.nationalinterest.org.
32 J. Stephens and D. B. Ottway, 'Afghan Roots Keep Advisor Firmly in the Inner Circle', *Washington Post*, 23 Nov. 2001.
33 Z. Khalilzad, *From Containment to Global Leadership?* (Santa Monica, 1995), pp. 15, 19, 21, 25.
34 Project for the New American Century, *Rebuilding America's Defenses*, Sept. 2000, www.newamericancentury.org, pp. 4, i.
35 *National Security Strategy*, pp. 26, 27.
36 Ibid., pp. 1, 30.
37 Project for the New American Century, *Rebuilding America's Defenses*, p. 8.
38 Quoted in Bacevich, *American Empire*, p. 223.
39 W. M. Arkin, 'Secret Plan Outlines the Unthinkable', *Los Angeles Times*, 10 Mar. 2002.
40 *National Security Strategy*, p. 29.
41 Priest, *The Mission*, p. 14.
42 Ibid., p. 17.
43 Ibid., ch. 3 (quotations from pp. 74, 70). See also Bacevich, *American Empire*, ch. 7.
44 Fallows, 'The Unilateralist'.

45 For two very different assessments of the military efficacy of strategic air power, compare Luttwak, *Strategy*, ch. 12, and Mearsheimer, *The Tragedy of Great Power Politics*, pp. 96–110.

46 'Secretary Rumsfeld Speaks on "Twenty-First Century" Transformation of the US Armed Forces', 31 Jan. 2002. Rumsfeld's revised version of American military doctrine is set out in Department of Defense, *Quadriennial Defense Review Report*, Sept. 2001. Both documents are available at www.defenselink.mil.

47 For the disputes between Rumsfeld and his generals, see S. M. Hersh, 'Offense and Defense', *New Yorker*, 7 Apr. 2003.

48 E. Luttwak, 'Dawn of a New Kind of War', *Sunday Telegraph*, 23 Mar. 2003.

49 Quoted in O. Burkeman, 'Shock Tactics', *Guardian*, 25 Mar. 2003.

50 Quoted in Fitzgerald, 'George Bush and the World', p. 84.

51 R. Perle, 'Thank God for the Death of the UN', *Guardian*, 21 Mar. 2003.

52 A. Lieven, 'The New Cold War', *London Review of Books*, 4 Oct. 2001, pp. 10, 12.

53 R. Kagan, *Paradise and Power* (London, 2003), pp. 27, 37.

54 Ibid., pp. 58, 73.

55 Cooper, 'The Post-Modern State'.

56 Kagan, *Paradise and Power*, p. 76. It is, of course, not true that the EU has transcended national antagonisms: see especially Alan Milward's classic *The European Rescue of the Nation-State* (London, 1994).

4 The Geopolitics of Oil

1 T. E. Ricks, 'Briefing Depicted Saudis as Enemies', *Washington Post*, 6 Aug. 2002, and L. Murawiec, 'Taking Saudi out of Arabia', Defense Policy Board, 10 July 2002, appendix to J. Shafer, 'The PowerPoint that Rocked the Pentagon', *Slate*, 7 Aug. 2002, www.slate.msn.com.

2 M. Ledeen, 'The Real Foe is Middle East Tyranny', *Financial Times*, 24 Sept. 2002. Conrad Burns, a Republican Congressman, argues for partnership with Russia as an alternative source of oil: 'America must Wean itself off Saudi Oil', *Financial Times*, 11 Oct. 2002.

3 Quoted in Yergin, *The Prize*, pp. 404–5.

4 Quoted in G. Achcar, *The Clash of Barbarisms*, p. 33; see ibid., ch. 2, for an important analysis of the Saudi regime and its relationship to both the US and radical Islamism.

5 Quoted in Yergin, *The Prize*, p. 702.

6 Quoted in Achcar, *The Clash of Barbarisms*, p. 35.

7 Murawiec, 'Taking Saudi out of Arabia'.

8 D. Gardner, 'Living with the Wolf', *Financial Times*, 17 Feb. 1998.

9 R. Khalaf, 'A Troubled Friendship', *Financial Times*, 22 Aug. 2002.

10 Murawiec, 'Taking Saudi out of Arabia'.

11 W. Kristol and R. Kagan, 'Remember the Bush Doctrine', *Weekly Standard*, 15 Apr. 2002.

12 Quoted in J. Lobe, 'A Right-Wing Blueprint for the Middle East', 4 Apr. 2002, www.alternet.org.

13 G. Friedman, 'The Region after Iraq', 6 Feb. 2003, www.stratfor.com.

14 M. Ledeen, 'The End of the Beginning', *Spectator*, 12 Apr. 2003, pp. 14, 15.

15 H. Batatu, *Syria's Peasantry, the Descendants of the Lesser Notables, and their Politics* (Princeton, 1999), pp. 289–300, and A. Shlaim, *The Iron Wall* (London, 2001), pp. 340–7.

16 See, on the arguments over whether to go to the UN, Woodward, *Bush at War*, Epilogue.

17 Quoted in Fidler and Baker, 'America's Democratic Imperialists'.

18 Ibid.

19 The ferment of mass struggles and radical politics under the Hashemite monarchy and the 1958 Revolution are vividly evoked in Hanna Batatu's classic work, *The Old Social Classes and the Revolutionary Movements of Iraq* (Princeton, 1978).

20 A. Lieven, 'A Trap of their Own Making', *London Review of Books*, 8 May 2003, p. 19.

21 Woodward, *Bush at War*, p. 341.

22 See, for example, J. Tatom, 'Iraq's Oil is Not America's Objective', *Financial Times*, 13 Feb. 2003.

23 S. Bromley, *American Hegemony and World Oil* (Cambridge, 1991), p. 86.

24 Yergin, *The Prize*, p. 541.

25 Speech at Marxism 2002, London, July 2002. George W. Bush owes his claims to belong to the American West to his father's decision in the late 1940s to move to Texas and enter the oil industry: Yergin, *The Prize*, pp. 753–4.
26 Lieven, 'The Push to War', p. 8.
27 *Reliable, Affordable, and Environmentally Sound Energy for America's Future: Report of the National Energy Policy Group*, May 2001. www.whitehouse.gov, quotations from pp. x, xv, 8-5.
28 Ibid., pp. 8-3, 8-16, 8-14.
29 M. T. Klare, 'Resources', in Feffer, *Power Trip*, p. 58.
30 R. Lapper, 'US Right Scents a New "Axis of Evil" in Latin America', *Financial Times*, 23 Oct. 2002.
31 Brzezinski, *The Grand Chessboard*, ch. 5 (quotation from p. 124).
32 Klare, 'Resources', pp. 57–8. The Bush administration is also seeking military bases on the west coast of Africa, whose oil reserves are expected to become increasingly important in meeting US energy needs.
33 See, for example, 'Don't Mention the O-Word – Iraq's Oil', *The Economist*, 14 Sept. 2002.
34 M. Renner, 'Post-Saddam Iraq: Linchpin of a New World Oil Order', in Sifry and Cerf, *The Iraq War Reader*, p. 584.

5 Collision of Empires

1 Bacevich, *American Empire*, p. 243.
2 N. Ferguson, 'Welcome to the New Imperialism', *Guardian*, 31 Oct. 2001.
3 Priest, *The Mission*, p. 30.
4 See for a recent argument for this conclusion that is all the more remarkable in the light of the author's belief that American military power can serve progressive goals, F. Halliday, 'The Persistence of Imperialism', in M. Rupert and H. Smith, eds, *Globalization and Historical Materialism* (London, 2002). See also Bensaïd, *Le Nouvel International-isme*, part 2. Two important discussions of imperialism in the transhistorical sense are M. Doyle, *Empires* (Ithaca, 1986), and E. M. Wood, *Empire of Capital* (London, 2003).
5 E. H. Carr, *The Twenty Years' Crisis* (London, 1939), H. Morgenthau, *Politics among Nations*, R. O. Keohane, ed.,

Neorealism and its Critics (New York, 1986), and Mearsheimer, *The Tragedy of Great Power Politics*.

6 M. Hardt and T. Negri, *Empire* (Cambridge, Mass., 2000), pp. xii, 9, 190. David Held and Tony McGrew offer a more nuanced social democratic version of the same perspective in *Globalization/Anti-Globalization* (Cambridge, 2002).

7 M. Hardt, 'Folly of our Masters of the Universe', *Guardian*, 18 Dec. 2002.

8 A. Negri, 'The Order of War' (Nov. 2002), http://www. generation-online.org/negriwar.htm.

9 A. J. P. Taylor, *The Struggle for Mastery in Europe 1848–1918* (Oxford, 1971). See, for example, K. N. Waltz, 'The Continuity of International Politics', in Booth and Dunne, *Worlds in Collision*.

10 J. J. Mearsheimer, 'Hearts and Minds', *National Interest*, 69 (2002).

11 A. Callinicos, *Making History* (Cambridge, 1987), chs 3–5. John Lewis Gaddis stresses the influence of ideology on Cold War decision-making: *We Know Now* (Oxford, 1997).

12 Mearsheimer, *The Tragedy of Great Power Politics*, chs 2, 4 and 7 (quotation from p. 40). Mearsheimer's fellow realist Robert Gilpin explicitly equates hegemony with imperial rule: see *War and Change in World Politics* (Cambridge, 1981), p. 29. For a critical assessment of Mearsheimer's analysis, see P. Gowan, 'A Calculus of Power', *New Left Review*, series II, 16 (2002).

13 Bromley, *American Hegemony and World Oil*, pp. 239, 241.

14 N. Bukharin, *Imperialism and World Economy* (London, 1972). Of course, economic rivalries among states predate the epoch of imperialism: access to the loot of empire was a crucial stake in the struggles between the European powers from the sixteenth century onwards. But only in the case of Holland and later England did the contestants operate from capitalist economic bases – something that gave them an important advantage over their absolutist rivals. In a sense, what happened in the nineteenth century was that the Anglo-Dutch model was generalized in the context of mass indus-trialization and the increasing organization of capital. See A. Callinicos, 'Bourgeois Revolutions and Historical Material-ism', in P. McGarr and A. Callinicos, *Marxism and the Great French Revolution* (London, 1993). I explore the contem-

porary relevance of the Marxist theory of imperialism further in 'Periodizing Capitalism and Analysing Imperialism', in R. Albritton et al., eds, *Phases of Capitalist Development* (Houndmills, 2001), 'Marxism and Global Governance', in D. Held and A. McGrew, eds, *Governing Globalization* (Cambridge, 2002), and *An Anti-Capitalist Manifesto*, pp. 50–65. Chris Harman has made an important contribution to this subject in 'Analysing Imperialism', *International Socialism*, series 2, 99 (2003).

15 See Ahmed Rashid's account of the recent economic and geopolitical conflicts over Afghanistan, *Taliban: Islam, Oil and the New Great Game in Central Asia* (London, 2000).

16 For a systematic analysis, see J. Rees, 'Imperialism: Globalization, the State and War', *International Socialism*, series 2, 93 (2001).

17 P. Kennedy, *The Rise of the Anglo-German Antagonism, 1860–1914* (London, 1980).

18 See, for example, I. Kershaw, *Hitler 1936–1945: Nemesis* (London, 2000), ch. 5, and pp. 400–7, 517, 528–30.

19 Therefore, unlike Giovanni Arrighi, who argues 'that the modern inter-state system' is characterized by 'the constant opposition of the capitalist and territorialist logics of power', *The Long Twentieth Century* (London, 1994), p. 36, I see economic and geopolitical competition as two forms – each with their own distinct and changing structure – of the more general logic of capitalist competition, forms that may mutually reinforce each other, but can also come into conflict.

20 Bacevich, *American Empire*, esp. ch. 4. The starting point for discussion of contemporary American economic strategy is P. Gowan, *The Global Gamble* (London, 1999), part 1.

21 There are good discussions of US global strategy in Mearsheimer, *The Tragedy of Great Power Politics*, ch. 7, and G. Friedman and M. Lebard, *The Coming War with Japan* (New York, 1991), chs 1 and 9. The latter book is saner, and more wide-ranging than its title suggests.

22 Gaddis, *Strategies of Containment*, pp. 4–9.

23 A. D. Harvey, *Collision of Empires: Britain in Three World Wars 1793–1945* (London, 1992), pp. 97–102 (quotation from p. 102 n28).

24 Quoted in V. G. Kiernan, *European Empires from Conquest to Collapse, 1815–1960* (London, 1982), p. 200; see also ibid., pp. 196–200.

25 Mearsheimer, *The Tragedy of Great Power Politics*, p. 236. The British counterpart, on a much smaller geographical scale, was the subordination of the whole of the British Isles to the English monarchy: the possibility that hostile powers might try to use Irish discontent to turn London's flank was demonstrated in both the French Revolutionary Wars and the First World War.

26 Quoted ibid., p. 238.

27 Quoted in A. Roberts, *Salisbury: Victorian Titan* (London, 1999), p. 617. Two years later Salisbury was embroiled in another near-war crisis with a liberal democracy, this time France, over control of the Nile valley: ibid., ch. 41.

28 Mearsheimer, *The Tragedy of Great Power Politics*, p. 246. The final chapter came in 1940–1, when the US supplied Britain with destroyers and other equipment, in exchange for control over the main British naval bases in the Western Hemisphere. 'In effect,' comment Friedman and Lebard, 'what the US did was to take advantage of British desperation to throw the Royal Navy out of the Western Atlantic', *The Coming War with Japan*, p. 24.

29 Kissinger, *Diplomacy*, p. 224.

30 G. Arrighi et al., 'The Transformation of Business Enterprise', in G. Arrighi and B. Silver et al., *Chaos and Governance in the Modern World System* (Minneapolis, 1999), pp. 127, 126.

31 G. Arrighi et al., 'Geopolitics and High Finance', in Arrighi and Silver et al., *Chaos and Governance in the Modern World System*, p. 83.

32 See G. Ingham, *Capitalism Divided? The City and Industry in British Social Development* (Houndmills, 1984).

33 M. Barrett Brown, *The Economics of Imperialism* (Harmondsworth, 1974), table 13, p. 176. Peter Gowan mistakenly perceives a further difference here, arguing that while British imperialism rested on the 'exploitative subjugation of pre-capitalist societies', American capitalism could only develop 'through dominance within the rest of the advanced capitalist core', 'A Calculus of Power', p. 63. This contrast is hard to reconcile with the fact that between 1860

and 1913 the largest single recipient of British overseas investment was the US, hardly a pre-capitalist society: Barrett Brown, *The Economics of Imperialism*, table 17, pp. 190–1; see also M. Barrett Brown, 'Away with All Great Arches', *New Left Review*, series I, 167 (1988).

34 G. Arrighi, 'Tracking Global Turbulence', *New Left Review*, series II, 20 (2003), p. 54 and n95.

35 For further analysis, see Brenner, *The Boom and the Bubble* and 'Towards the Precipice', *London Review of Books*, 6 Feb. 2003.

36 M. Wolf, 'Asia is Footing the Bill for American Guns and Butter', *Financial Times*, 19 Feb. 2003.

37 J. Plender, 'The Sinews of War are Asian', *Financial Times*, 21 Mar. 2003.

38 Arrighi et al., 'Geopolitics and High Finance', p. 38.

39 G. Arrighi and B. Silver, 'Conclusion', in Arrighi and Silver et al., *Chaos and Governance in the Modern World System*, p. 275 (emphasis in the original).

40 See especially Arrighi, *The Long Twentieth Century*.

41 For an appraisal of the strategy involved in the huge increase in US military spending that followed the outbreak of the Korean War, see F. Block, 'Economic Instability and Military Strength: The Paradox of the 1950 Rearmament Decision' (1980) in Ikenberry, *American Foreign Policy*. My analysis in this and the following paragraphs is heavily indebted to M. Kidron, *Western Capitalism since the War* (Harmondsworth, 1970) and C. Harman, *Explaining the Crisis* (London, 1984). The theory of the 'permanent arms economy' developed in these works is an essential supplement and corrective to the account of growing competition and declining profitability offered by Robert Brenner in 'The Economics of Global Turbulence'.

42 G. Duménil and D. Levy, 'Néolibéralisme-néomilitarisme', *Actuel Marx*, 33 (2003), p. 90.

43 Brenner, *The Boom and the Bubble*, p. 222.

44 R. Layard, 'Britain will Pay the Price of Exclusion', *Financial Times*, 15 Oct. 2002. The difference between the two measures is important because workers in the US and Britain work much longer hours than they do on the continent, so that productivity measured by output per head

favours some countries and output per hour worked favours others.

45 *Financial Times*, 23 Oct. 2002.

46 Ibid., 23 Apr. 2003.

47 Arrighi, 'Tracking Global Turbulence', pp. 53–4.

48 Gowan evokes the possibility of such a development: 'A Calculus of Power', pp. 66–7.

49 See the careful assessment of the strengths and weaknesses of US capitalism in the 1990s in Brenner, *The Boom and the Bubble*, ch. 9.

50 For an illuminating analysis, see R. T. Murphy, 'Japan's Economic Crisis', *New Left Review*, series II, 1 (2000).

51 For example, B. Scowcroft, 'Don't Attack Saddam', *Wall Street Journal*, 15 Aug. 2002.

52 R. Holbrooke, 'High Road to Baghdad', *Guardian*, 29 Aug. 2002.

53 R. Kagan, 'Multilateralism American Style', *Washington Post*, 13 Sept. 2002.

54 For Brzezinski's views, see, for example, 'Right and Wrong Ways to Wage a War', *International Herald Tribune*, 19 Aug. 2002.

55 'Remarks by the President in Address to the United Nations General Assembly, New York, New York', 12 Sept. 2002, www.whitehouse.gov.

56 Brzezinski, *The Grand Chessboard*, pp. 55–6.

57 J. Harding, ' "Legitimacy of American Leadership" Eroded', *Financial Times*, 4 Mar. 2003.

58 Huntington, 'The Lonely Superpower'.

59 On the latter aspect, see Robert Keohane's analysis, 'The Public Delegitimation of Terrorism and Coalition Politics', in Booth and Dunne, *Worlds in Collision*.

60 See Milward, *The European Rescue of the Nation State*, and A. Callinicos, 'The Contradictions of European Monetary Union', in W. Bonefeld, ed., *The Politics of Europe* (Houndmills, 2001).

61 *Financial Times*, 24 Jan. 2003.

62 'The Divided West: Part Two', *Financial Times*, 28 May 2003.

63 For a detailed critique of British global policy see M. Curtis, *Web of Deceit* (London, 2003).

64 G. Friedman, 'American Isolation and the European Reality', 12 Mar. 2003, www.stratfor.com.

65 P. Stephens, 'A Divided Europe will be Easy for America to Rule', *Financial Times*, 23 May 2003.

66 Huntington, 'The Lonely Superpower'.

67 I have benefited from hearing a presentation that stressed this point by Claude Serfati at the International Forum organized by the Mouvement pour le Socialisme in Lausanne, 16–17 May 2003.

68 Perry Anderson makes a similar judgement (though he draws much too pessimistic conclusions about the antiwar movement): 'Force and Consent', *New Left Review*, series II, 17 (2002).

69 Pogge, *World Poverty and Human Rights*, pp. 97–8.

70 United Nations Development Programme, *Human Development Report 1999* (New York, 1999), p. 3.

71 W. Easterly, 'The Lost Decades: Developing Countries' Stagnation in spite of Policy Reform', *Journal of Economic Growth*, 6 (2001), p. 154.

72 Pogge, *World Poverty and Human Rights*, p. 2.

73 *Guardian*, 10 Apr. 2003.

The epigraph at the end of the book is from Ammianus Marcellinus, *The Later Roman Empire*, ed. and trans. W. Hamilton (Harmondsworth, 1986), XIV.11.

Index

Abdullah, Crown Prince 84
Achcar, Gilbert 82, 133n, 143n
Acheson, Dean 66
Afghanistan 7, 8, 9–10, 22, 34,
    36, 51, 55, 64, 68, 73,
    74–5, 82–3, 89, 92, 105,
    107, 127, 146n
Africa 36, 95, 144n
African National Congress 13
Agamben, Giorgio 6
Agreed Framework (1994) 22–3
al-Assad, Bashar 87, 90–1
al-Assad, Hafez 87
al-Qaeda 10, 11, 13, 14, 37, 51,
    53, 70, 81, 89, 91
Albright, Madeleine 63, 84,
    120
Alexander the Great 3, 99
Ali, Tariq 133n
Amal 87
Ammianus Marcellinus 1–3, 131
Amnesty International 24
Anderson, Perry 150n
Angola 45
Anti-Ballistic Missile Treaty
    (1972) 17, 72, 89
Anti-Comintern Pact (1936) 14
Antiwar protests (15 February
    2003) 7, 40, 130

Arab Ba'ath Socialist Party 4,
    15, 19, 27, 43, 75, 90,
    91
Armitage, Richard L. 50
Arrighi, Giovanni 106, 109,
    110, 111, 113–14, 117–18,
    127, 146n
Australia 119
'Axis of evil' 14–18, 19, 22–3,
    84
Azerbaijan 97

Ba'athism see Arab Ba'ath
    Socialist Party
Bacevich, Andrew J. 57, 61, 63,
    99, 106
Baghdad 1, 3, 5, 19, 52, 75, 92,
    98, 120
Baker, Gerald 88
Baker, III, James A. 45, 90,
    119–20
Balkan War (1999) 17, 35, 55,
    61–2, 63, 65, 89
Barr, Kenneth 109
Batatu, Hanna 143n
Bechtel Corp 33
Beirut 11–12
Belgium 65
Bensaïd, Daniel 41

bin Laden, Osama 8–9, 10, 13, 51, 70, 83, 84
Blair, Tony 3, 4, 17, 20–1, 35–41, 62, 92, 119, 120, 136n
blitzkrieg 75, 76
Block, Fred 148n
Bobbitt, Philip 30–2, 33
Bolton, John R. 14, 47, 49, 50, 76
Bosnia 61
Bremer, L. Paul 33, 98
Brenner, Robert 115, 117, 148n, 149n
Britain 3, 12–13, 16, 17, 20–1, 25, 33, 36, 63, 65, 69, 75, 76, 79, 81, 86, 91, 99, 102, 103, 105, 106–12, 114, 115, 119–27, 147–8n
British Broadcasting Corporation (BBC) 13, 21
Bromley, Simon 93, 98, 104
Brzezinski, Zbigniew 9–10, 60–1, 62–3, 64, 70, 83, 96, 120–1, 123, 140n, 149n
The Grand Chessboard 62–3
Bukharin, N. I. 104
Bulgaria 123
Burns, Conrad 142n
Bush, George H. W. 19–20, 44–7, 54, 59, 68, 87, 90, 99, 119–20, 127, 129, 134n, 144n
Bush, George W. 3–6, 8, 9, 11, 13, 14, 17, 19, 24, 25, 26, 27, 28–9, 30, 31, 35, 36, 38–9, 41, 42–8, 51–3, 54, 55, 57, 58, 64–5, 68, 70, 72, 73, 74, 77, 80, 83, 88–9, 92, 94, 99, 100, 102, 103, 105, 112, 113, 116, 119–20, 124, 126, 129, 144n
Bush Doctrine 6, 42–4, 66, 102, 105, 129

Cambodia 92
Canada 18, 94
capitalism 6, 24, 27, 29–34, 57, 67, 100, 101–6, 109–110, 126, 127–30, 145–6n, 147–8n
Carlyle Group 90
Carr, E. H. 101
Carroll, Philip 33
Carter, Jimmy 9–10, 82–3, 116, 118
Carter Doctrine 82
Caspian Sea 95–7
Castro, Fidel 96, 109
Central America 45, 85, 109
Central Asia 24, 58, 62, 72, 73, 95, 96–7, 98, 105, 122
Central Command 73, 83
Central and Eastern Europe 24, 27, 43, 58, 61–2, 85, 123–4
Central Intelligence Agency (CIA) 9–10, 28, 45, 46, 135n
Chace, James 66
Chalabi, Ahmad 28, 51
Chávez, Hugo 96
Chechnya 122
Cheney, Richard B. 31–2, 45–6, 47, 68, 88, 89, 94–5
Cheney report (2001) 94–5
Chevron 94
China 22, 29, 33, 58, 59–60, 63, 67–8, 71, 72, 95, 96, 98, 102, 113, 115, 119, 127, 140n
Chirac, Jacques 121–3
Chomsky, Noam 7, 11, 16
Christian fascists (Lebanon) 11–12, 87
Christian fundamentalism 49
Churchill, Winston 81
Cleveland, Grover 108
Clinton, William J. 16–17, 22, 31, 46–7, 50, 54, 55, 58, 60, 61–4, 67, 70, 72–3, 84,

89, 96, 97, 99, 116, 120, 121, 127–8
Cold War 5, 24, 26, 42, 44, 45, 55–6, 57, 58–9, 60, 61, 66–7, 68, 72, 74, 101, 107, 112, 114–16, 126, 127, 128, 141n, 145n
Colombia 96
competition
  economic 59, 100, 104–6, 112, 114–18, 126–7, 145n, 146n
  geopolitical 29–30, 57–9, 67–72, 100–6, 110, 112, 114–18, 121–7, 129, 145n, 146n
Congress (US) 9, 51, 66, 72
containment 42–4, 66, 92
Cooper, Robert 40, 79
Copenhagen 107
Ctesiphon 1–3
Cuba 14, 96, 109
Cumings, Bruce 134n

Daalder, Ivo H. 88
Davis, Mike 94
Defense Planning Guidance (1992) 45–6
Defense Policy Board 47, 80–1, 84
democracy 4–5, 15, 23–34, 48, 85–6, 93, 108
Democratic Party 43, 76
Democratic Republic of the Congo 129
Department of Defense (US) 28, 45–6, 47, 48, 52, 55, 64, 65, 72, 75–6, 97, 99, 112, 115, 118, 126, 129, 130
Derrida, Jacques 15–16
Disarmament Conference (1932) 107
Dower, John 26
Dresden 107
Drury, Shadia 138n

Eagleburger, Lawrence S. 119–20
East Asia 22–3, 60, 67, 69, 72, 77, 100, 113, 114, 116, 118
Easterly, William 128
economic crisis 26–7, 59, 61, 115–16, 148n
Egypt 5, 13, 85, 90, 119
End of History 24, 40, 67, 79
Enron 94
Eurasia 55, 57, 59, 62–3, 69, 103, 105, 106, 107, 120, 140n
European Union 40, 61, 63, 77–9, 110, 116, 117, 119–27, 142n
ExxonMobil 98

Fallows, James 54, 74, 76
Feith, Douglas J. 47, 49
Ferguson, Niall 99
Fidler, Stephen 88
Financial Times 33, 42, 53, 85, 96
First World War 5, 35, 55, 104, 111, 112
Fitzgerald, Frances 47
Ford, Gerald R. 46, 58, 119
France 18, 25, 35, 44, 65, 79, 102, 117, 119–27, 147n
Franks, General Tommy 73
free trade 29, 36, 37–8, 55, 106
Freedman, Lawrence 23
Friedman, George 52–3, 59, 86, 123, 146n, 147n
  The Coming War with Japan 59
Fukuyama, Francis 24, 79

Gaddis, John Lewis 145n
Genoa protests (July 2001) 36
Georgia 97
Geras, Norman 133

Germany 4, 14, 18, 25–7, 35,
    55, 58, 61, 63, 65, 66,
    67–8, 79, 98, 102, 105–6,
    107, 112, 114, 117, 119–27
Gibbon, Edward 1, 2
Gilpin, Robert 145n
Global Crossing 47
global warming 17, 36, 39, 94,
    129
globalization 36–9, 74, 99,
    101–2, 104, 130
Goebbels, Josef 53
Gorbachev, M. S. 116
Gowan, Peter 146n, 147–8n
Greece 66
Greenspan, Alan 117
Greider, William 38
Growth and Stability Pact (1996)
    125–6
Guantanamo Bay 8, 41
Gulf War (1980–8) 14–15,
    19–20
Gulf War (1991) 19, 45, 47, 52,
    54, 83, 119–20

Haass, Richard N. 52
Haiti 89, 109
Halabja massacre (1988) 19
Halliburton 31–2
Halliday, Fred 144n
Hamas 81
Hamburg 107
Hardt, Michael 101–2
Harman, Chris 146n, 148n
hegemony 30, 59, 62–3, 69–72,
    74, 93, 95, 103–4, 105,
    106, 112, 114, 122, 145n
Held, David 145n
Hersh, Seymour 21
Hiroshima 76, 107
Hisaeda, Shuji 109
Hitchens, Christopher 34, 35,
    48
Hitler, Adolf 105–6, 107
Hizbollah 81, 87, 91

Holbrooke, Richard C. 120
Hoon, Geoff 3
Hui, Po-keung 110
Human Rights Watch 24, 82
humanitarian intervention 35,
    62, 92, 100
Huntington, Samuel P. 16–17,
    19, 121, 126
Hussein, Saddam 4, 11, 16,
    19–20, 23, 27, 33, 34, 35,
    39, 44, 49, 50, 51, 52, 53,
    68, 70, 75–6, 80, 83, 85,
    86, 87, 89, 91, 97, 120,
    129, 134n, 135n

Ibn Saud, King 82
Ignatieff, Michael 39
Ikenberry, G. John 55
imperialism 6, 39–41, 57, 62–3,
    73–4, 98, 99–127, 129–30,
    144n, 145–6n
India 22, 71, 96, 107, 111
International Atomic Energy
    Agency 21
International Criminal Court 17,
    77
International Monetary Fund
    55, 106, 117, 126
International Rescue Committee
    129
Iran 14–15, 27–8, 43, 68, 72,
    81, 87, 90–2, 97
Iranian Revolution (1978–9) 20,
    82–3
Iraq 3–5, 10, 13, 14–15, 16,
    17–21, 23, 25, 26, 27–8,
    32–4, 39–40, 43–4, 45, 48,
    49, 50–3, 55, 63, 65, 68,
    72, 74, 75–6, 81, 82, 83,
    85, 86, 87, 89, 90–2, 97–8,
    107, 109, 112–13, 119–27,
    130
Iraq Liberation Act 1998 51
Iraq Museum 3
Iraqi Communist Party 27, 91

Iraqi National Congress (INC)
    28, 48, 135n
Iraqi Revolution (1958) 28,
    143n
Ireland 36, 147n
Islam 4, 81, 83
Islamic Jihad 81
Islamism 9–10, 27, 67, 68, 81,
    83, 91, 119, 143n
Israel 11–12, 22, 36, 41, 45,
    48–50, 81, 85, 87, 91, 92,
    127
Italy 14, 117, 124

Jackson, Bruce 123
Japan 4, 14, 22–3, 25–7, 55, 59,
    60, 61, 63, 66, 67, 93, 98,
    107, 113, 114–18, 126
Jefferson, Thomas 107
Jenin 85
Jerusalem Post 49
Johnson, Chalmers 9
Johnson, Lyndon B. 38
Jordan 28, 49
Julian, Emperor 1–4

Kabul 34, 65, 89
Kagan, Robert 63, 77–9, 85,
    120
Kaplan, Lawrence F. 25, 57, 72,
    134n, 141n
Karimov, Islam 24
Karzai, Hamid 34, 89
Kazakhstan 97
Keegan, John 3
Kellogg, Brown & Root 32
Kelly, David 21
Kennan, George F. 43
Kennedy, John F. 57
Keohane, Robert O. 149n
Keynesianism 30, 39, 56, 126
Khalilzad, Zalmay 50, 51,
    68–70
Kidron, Michael 148n
Kim Jong-Il 23, 70

Kissinger, Henry A. 45, 46, 49,
    57–8, 63, 69, 70, 109, 120
Klare, Michael T. 95–7
Kolko, Gabriel 139n
Korb, Lawrence J. 83
Korean War (1950–3) 22, 107,
    116, 148n
Kosovo 35, 61, 62
Kristol, William 25, 50, 57, 85,
    134n, 141n
Kupchan, Charles A. 88, 89
Kurdish nationalism 27, 91
Kuwait 64, 83, 86, 119, 129
Kyoto protocol (1997) 17, 39,
    77, 89, 94
Kyrgyzstan 97

Labour Party 36
LaRouche, Lyndon 80
Latin America 24, 96, 109
Layard, Richard 117
League of Nations 109, 120
Lebanese National Movement
    87
Lebanon 11–12, 81, 87–8, 91
Lebard, Meredith 146, 147
Ledeen, Michael A. 81, 86–7
Lemann, Nicholas 51
Liberal Democratic Party (Japan)
    26
liberalism 55–7, 103, 104
Liberty 12–13
Libya 14, 72
Liebknecht, Karl 35
Lieven, Anatole 54, 77, 92, 94
Likud 49
Lind, Michael 47–8, 138n
Lloyd George, David 107
Lodge, Sr, Henry Cabot, 108
Louisiana Purchase (1803)
    108
Lula da Silva, Luiz Inácio 96
Luttwak, Edward N. 55, 75,
    139n
Luxemburg, Rosa 35

Maastricht Treaty (1991) 123, 125
Macedonian Empire 99, 107
McGrew, Anthony 145n
Mackinder, Sir Halford 140n
Mandela, Nelson 13
Mann, Michael 1
Marshall Plan (1947) 56, 66, 111
Marxism 100, 104–6
Mattera, Philip 32–3
Mazar-e-Sharif 74–5
Mead, Walter Russell 139n
Mearsheimer, John J. 19–20, 60, 101, 102–4, 107–8, 145n, 146n
Mecca 81
Medina 81
Mesopotamia 1–3 *see also* Iraq
Mexico 18, 94, 108, 109
Middle East 4, 6, 19–20, 21, 25, 34, 43–4, 48–50, 79, 80–98, 105, 120
  peace process 45, 49, 85
military expenditure 38, 89, 112–13, 115, 116–17, 125–6, 128–9, 148n
military power 50, 54, 61, 64, 65, 70–6, 103, 107, 112–18, 125–7, 144n
Milošević, Slobodan 62
Milward, Alan 142n
Ministry of Defence (UK) 20, 21
Mongol Empire 3, 99
Monroe Doctrine 108, 109
Morgenthau, Hans J. 18, 100
Morocco 13
Mubarak, Hosni 5, 13, 90
mujahedin 9–10, 68, 83
multilateralism 17, 55–6, 61–4, 78–9, 88, 120, 126–7, 140n
Murawiec, Laurent 80, 84, 85
Murdoch, Rupert 50
Musharraf, Pervez 24

Nagasaki 76
National Interest, The 47
National Missile Defense 47, 72
National Security Council 47, 51, 66
National Security Strategy of the United States of America, The 6, 29–30, 33, 65, 70–2
Negri, Antonio 101–2
neoconservatism 6, 23–34, 47–53, 54, 64–93, 138n
neoliberalism 29–34, 35, 37–9, 106, 118, 127–30
Netanyahu, Binyamin 49
New York 5, 12, 36, 51, 90
New York Times 7, 45, 82
Nicaragua 45, 109
Niger 21
Nixon, Richard M. 49, 58, 115
Noriega, Manuel 109
North Atlantic Treaty Organization (Nato) 17, 61–2, 63, 64–5, 72, 102, 120, 123, 125
North East Asia *see* East Asia
North Korea 14–15, 22–3, 72
Northern Alliance 74–5
NSC-68 141n
Nuclear Non-Proliferation Treaty (1968) 22
Nuclear Posture Review (2002) 72
nuclear weapons 21–3, 72, 76, 91, 129
Nye, Joseph S. 140n

Office of Special Plans 48
oil 33, 86, 93–8, 105, 142n, 144n
Organization of Petroleum Exporting Countries (OPEC) 86, 97–8

Pakistan 22, 24, 68, 96, 126
Palestine 10, 36, 85
Palestine Liberation Organization
    12, 45, 81, 87
Panama 109
Pentagon 51
    all other references see
    Department of Defense
Perle, Richard N. 28, 47, 49,
    50, 76, 80–1
Persian Empire 1–4
Philippines 72
Plender, John 113
Pogge, Thomas W. 39, 128
poverty and inequality 36–9,
    128–9
Powell, Colin L. 47, 64, 88
Powell Doctrine 64
Priest, Dana 24, 72–4, 99
privatization 30, 32–3, 98,
    118
productivity 117–18, 148–9n
Project for the New American
    Century 6, 50–1, 70, 71
protectionism 39, 55, 77
Putin, V. V. 121–2

Qatar 126

Rai, Krishnendu 110
RAND Corporation 68, 80
Rashid, Ahmed 146n
Reagan, Ronald W. 45, 50, 57,
    63, 68, 74, 83, 116, 118,
    126, 134n
realism 57, 100–4, 134n
Rees, John 146n
regional military commands (US)
    73–4
Reifer, Thomas Ehrlich 110
Renner, Michael 98
Republican Party 38–9, 43,
    44–53, 54, 76, 77, 94
    see also neoconservatism

Rice, Condoleezza 44, 47, 52,
    55, 57, 65–6, 89, 94
rogue states 15–18, 19, 62, 67
Roman Empire 1–4, 74, 99,
    103, 107
Romania 123
Rome, Treaty of (1957) 122
Roosevelt, Franklin D. 38, 81–2,
    107
Rove, Karl 5
Roy, Arundhati 33
Royal Dutch-Shell 33, 98
Rumsfeld, Donald H. 19–20, 28,
    32, 33, 46–7, 50, 51, 53,
    65, 74–6, 81, 88, 89, 90,
    98, 99, 116, 123, 133n,
    134n, 138n, 142n
Runciman, David 136n
Russia 18, 22, 29, 33, 35, 44,
    58, 59, 60, 62, 63, 71, 72,
    79, 95, 102, 106, 119–27,
    142n
RWE/Thames Water 33

Sabra and Chatila massacres
    (1982) 11–12
St Malo agreement (1998)
    125
Salisbury, Robert Gascoyne-
    Cecil, 3rd Marquess of 108,
    147n
SALT II 46, 138n
Sandinistas 109
Sargon of Akkad 1, 100
Saudi Arabia 5, 13, 80–6, 88,
    90, 93, 94, 97, 119–27,
    143n
Schröder, Gerard 121–2
Scowcroft, Brent 119–20
Seattle protests (November 1999)
    130
Second World War 4, 5, 25, 43,
    56, 66, 81–2, 105–6, 107,
    111, 112, 114

Secret Intelligence Service 21
September 11 2001 5, 8–11, 12,
    13, 22, 34, 36, 44, 47, 48,
    51–3, 64–6, 70, 73, 77, 83,
    85, 89, 90, 95, 96, 102,
    103, 105, 122, 126, 127,
    128
Serbia 17, 61, 62
Serfati, Claude 150n
Shamir, Yitzhak 45
Sharon, Ariel 12, 49
Shulsky, Abram N. 48
Silver, Beverley 114, 127
Smith, Tony 56–7
Somalia 89
South Korea 22–3
Southern Europe 24, 55
Soviet Union 9–10, 26, 27, 43,
    45, 46, 55–6, 58, 60, 65,
    74, 82–3, 105–6, 107, 115,
    116, 122
Spain 124
Special Forces (US) 75
Stalin, J. V. 81
Stalingrad 105
State Department 20, 73
Stephens, Philip 124
Stratfor 52, 59, 86
Strauss, Leo 48, 138n
Suez 33, 118
Syria 14, 49, 72, 81, 86–8,
    90–2, 119–27

Taiwan 113
Taliban 10, 24, 34, 68, 105
Taylor, A. J. P. 102
Tel al-Za'atar massacre (1976)
    87
terrorism 9, 11–14, 36, 53, 67,
    119, 129
Terrorism Act 2000 12–13
Third Way 35–9
transformational warfare 74–5,
    142n
Trotskyism 47–8, 138n

Truman, Harry S. 56, 57, 66,
    82, 141n
Truman Doctrine (1947) 66, 82
Turkey 18, 27, 49, 65, 75, 86,
    119
Turkmenistan 68

Ullman, Harlan K. 76
unilateralism 16–18, 54, 63–5,
    77–9, 120, 127
United Nations 16–18, 21, 52,
    55, 64, 65, 76, 88, 98, 102,
    120, 143n
  Security Council 16–18, 19,
    21, 33, 43–44, 45, 52, 63,
    64, 76, 77, 119, 120, 122
United States 3, 5, 9, 13, 16–18,
    19–20, 21–3, 24, 25, 26,
    29, 33, 34, 37, 39–40,
    42–4, 49, 53, 54–98,
    99–100, 102, 103, 105,
    106–127, 134n, 143n, 144n,
    146n, 147n, 148n, 149n
University of Chicago 48, 68
Unocal 68
US Army 11, 12, 75
USA Patriot Act 12
Uzbekistan 24, 97, 126

Vedrine, Hubert 112
Venezuela 94, 96, 108
Vietnam War (1930–75) 7, 64,
    107, 115, 117, 128, 130
Vivendi Universal 33, 118

Wald, Alan 138n
Wall Street Journal 85–6
Walt, Stephen J. 19–20
Waltz, Kenneth N. 101
Walzer, Michael 34–5, 36
'war on terrorism' 5–7, 8–14,
    17, 36–9, 42–4, 64–6, 70,
    72, 96–7, 102–3, 113, 122,
    126, 128, 129
Washington DC 5, 12, 36, 51

Washington Post 52, 68, 72,
    138n
weapons of mass destruction
    (WMD) 18–23, 44, 52–3,
    90–1, 129
Weekly Standard, The 50, 51
Weinberger, Caspar W. 64
Western Asia 73, 89
Western Europe 56, 61, 69, 72,
    77, 93, 114–18
Western Hemisphere 55, 69,
    107–9, 147n
Wilson, Thomas Woodrow 55,
    109
Wolf, Martin 112
Wolfowitz, Paul D. 28, 46, 47,
    48, 50, 51, 67–8, 70, 88,
    89, 92

Woodward, Bob 46, 66, 92
Woolsey, R. James 5
World Bank 106, 128
World Trade Organization 39,
    126, 127
Wurmser, David 49

Xenophon 48

Yergin, Daniel 93
Yŏngbyŏn 22
Yugoslavia 35, 55, 59, 61, 62,
    74, 107

Zinni, General Anthony 73
Zoellick, Robert B. 50